ENVIRONMENT HOW INFLUENCES CONSUMER BEHAVIORS

JOHN LOK

Copyright © John Lok
All Rights Reserved.

ISBN 979-888591771-1

Contents

Preface

Introduction

The objective of macroeconomic behavioral methods is to control the short run behavior of an country's economy development. Is it useful to be applied to assist developing countries' economic development. If we think of stability as a situation in which the main macro variables are at a desired or target level. This book divides two parts, this first part, I shall explain how to apply economic methods to measure consumer shopping behavior as well as this second part, I shall explain how to apply economic methods to measure airport or airline passenger travelling service demand behavior. In first part , I shall explain whether macro or micro economic method is more easily to predict or measure when and how and why the developing country's consumer shopping desire to be rised or reduced. Can we apply macroeconomic behavioral methods to help developing countries to control current rate of inflation, output or productive rising levels. It is necessary for the developing countries' economy to adjust from its current situation of instability to the target stabilised position.

In fact, any developing countries' economic in instability problem is reflecting in high inflation, low output growth and a growing balance of payment deficit. I shall indicate reasons whether we can apply macroeconomic behavioral methods to help developing countries to measure why and how and when consumer behavior or desire to be rised or reduced.

This part researches whether macro economic can measure how social change to influence positive or negative factor will impact any countries' crime rate to be raised or reduced. Has it relationship between global macro economic environment and young unemployed people whose behaviors change, e.g. attempting stealing when they encounter long term unemployment suitation or attempting to sell illegal drug to earn income or performing anit-social damage behavior to influence convenient road transportation and working people need catch amy public transportation tools etc. traffic jam manual causing anti-social damage behavior? Is poor macro economic environment main factor to influence crime number increases ?

Readers can make more accurate analysis to judge whether macro or micro economic methods can measure when and how and why social crime behaviors occurs as well as social consumer consumption desire why is rasied or reduced easily after you read this book.

In the second part, I shall explain whether it is possible to predict travel behavioural consumption from psychology view and computer statistic view. Second, I shall indicate what factors can influence travel behavioural consumption, such as climate changing, renting travel car tools choice, the country's risk and safety. Then I shall indicate psychological factor to influence travel behavioural consumption, such as: push and pull psychological factor, expectation and motivation and attitude factor.

In this part, I shall general investigating methods to predict travel behavioural consumption, such as qualitative of travel behavioural method, advanced traveler information systems (ATIS) method, online tourism sale channel method, actively based patterns of urban population of travel behavioural prediction method, trip based versus activity based approaches of method. In the second part, I shall explain why the future travel age target will be the senior age group and I shall indicate how to use psychological method to predict travel behavioral consumption.

This part also researchs how airport management influences passengers consumption behavior. Nowadays, travellers enjoy to go to different countries to travel. In consumer psychological view, instead of the travelling agents' travelling e-ticket cheap and fast seats online booking service or walk in travelling travel agents travelling paper ticket purchase or attractive trip arrangement service to attract travelling consumers' choice.

In any countries, whether attractive airport appearance design, airport convenient public transportaton tools service, e.g. enough airport bus, taxi, train, tram , underground train , ferry etc. number supplying , which can let any foreign travellers find and choose any kinds of public transportaton tools to catch to arrive destinations when they arrive any countries' airports easily, different kinds of varoety of attractive product shops or food courts/ shops which can let airport passengers to sit down and choose any kinds of food to eat or they can choose any books, magazines, or stationerys or cigarettes, wine, toys , electronic products, e.g. desktop, laptop computers etc. products to consume for reading or using need in the airport's any restaurants or ships conveniently.

All these airports' intangible or tangible factors whether they can influence consumers' shopping desires in airports, even whether these both factors can attract or persuade many travellers prefer to choose to go to the country to travel and increase the country's travellers number. Concerning these two questions, my readers can earn more useful opinions to analyse whether any country's airport's image will have relationship to influence travellers' tourism choice and tourism consumption choice behavior , due to the country's airport's facility management , service, appearance design , convenient transportation, safety etc. important factors influence in order to assist to develop the country's tourism industry success in possible.

Does this travelling entertainment activities similar fee comparison factor influence any travellers choose to find the cheaper travelling entertainment activities arrangement provider? If travelling entertainment activities arrangement price is not the main factor to influence traveller individual choice. What other factors can influence traveller individual travelling entertainment activities arrangement choice? I shall explain what the other factors are influcenced traveller individual travelling entertainment arrangement choice.

The factors include that the cultural distance on satisfaction and travel intention factor, the lifestyle concept in travel behavioral factor, the business travellers motivation behavioral factor, the impacts of peer-to-peer accommodation use on travel patterns factor, factors influence local tourists decision-making be on choosing a destination factor, transportation, shopping centers, travelling destination facilities supplying factor, social media travelling networking sites promotion factor, traveller's travelling experience psychological factor, travelling service for disabled people's travelling need factor, green travel entertainment service for environment protection travelling environment need factor the impact of travel blogging on the tourist, traveller individual vacation destination choice factor, economic impact to the traveller individual sudden changing factor.

The second part , such as travel entertainment industry, nowadays global travelling entertainment activities are popular, some travellers like domestic travelling or some travellers like to catch airplanes to go to other countries travel. In consumer behavioral view point, when the consumer discovers the product's price is higher than the another product's price. Then, he/ she will usually to choose to buy the cheaper product, such as travel agent travelling entertainment activities arrangement service case, whether the travelling provider charges higher travelling entertainment activities arrangement service fee to compare the another similar travelling entertainment activities arrangement service provider. Does this travelling entertainment activities similar fee comparison factor influence any travellers choose to find the cheaper travelling entertainment activities arrangement provider? If travelling entertainment activities arrangement price is not the main factor to influence traveller individual choice. What other factors can influence traveller individual travelling entertainment activities arrangement choice? I shall explain what the other factors are influenced traveller individual travelling entertainment arrangement choice.

The factors include that the cultural distance on satisfaction and travel intention factor, the lifestyle concept in travel behavioral factor, the business travellers motivation behavioral factor, the impacts of peer-to-peer accommodation use on travel patterns factor, factors influence local tourists decision-making be on choosing a destination factor, transportation, shopping centers, travelling destination facilities supplying factor, social media travelling networking sites promotion factor, traveller's travelling experience psychological factor, travelling service for disabled people's travelling need factor, green travel entertainment service for environment protection travelling environment need factor the impact of travel blogging on the tourist, traveller individual vacation destination choice factor, economic impact to the traveller individual sudden changing factor.

Therefore, it brings these questions: How any why traveller individual travelling choice won't be influenced by travelling entertainment service price only? Does it mean the travelling entertainment service providers will not reduce their traveller number when they can respect or consider above factors to avoid to bring negative influence to traveller consumers, but they still change higher travelling entertainment arrangement service fee to them? Does this travelling entertainment activities similar fee comparison factor influence any travellers choose to find the cheaper travelling entertainment activities arrangement provider? If travelling entertainment activities arrangement price is not the main factor to influence traveller individual choice. What other factors can influence traveller individual travelling entertainment activities arrangement choice?

I shall explain what the other factors are influcenced traveller individual travelling entertainment arrangement choice.In my this part, I shall explain above factors how to influence traveller individual behavior to let readers can predict traveller individual behavior more accurately.

Prologue

Emotional labor factor

Airports service environment
factor

Lean maintenance repair
and manual error factor

Influence of airside and off
airport to airport geographical
choice factor

Influencing air connectivity
to service quality factor
How to measure and rise airline
service quality

reference

Chapter 6
Economic environment
influence traveller behavior

Prediction travel behavioral consumption
from psychology view and computer statistic
view. p.220-269

Whether climate change can influence
travelling behaviours.
Future travel consumption behavior
Whether individual habitual behaviour can influence travelling
behaviour: e.g. renting
travel transportation tools
How to determine future travel behavior
from past travel experience and perceptions
of risk and safety for the benefits to travel consumers?

What is push and pull factors to influence

any traveler who chooses where is whose
preferable travelling destination.

Why expectation, motivation and attitude factor
can influence travelling behaviour.

What methods can predict future travel behavioural consumption

How to use qualitative of travel behavioural
method to predict future travel consumption.
How to apply advanced traveler information
systems (ATIS) to predict future travelling
behaviour.
How does online tourism sale channel can
influence traveling consumption of behaviour.
Actively based patterns of urban population of
travel behavioural prediction method.
What is trip based versus activity based
approaches?
Why senior age will be main travelling target.
Psychological method to predict
travel behavioural consumption.
reference
Cultural distance on satisfaction and
respect travel intention
Lifestyle factor influences travel
behavior
How any why peer-to-peer
accommodation can impact
business tourism pattern
Factors influence local tourists'
destination choice
Tourist individual driving behavior
how to impact travel behavior
What are usually travel behaviors
and attitudes to disabled tourists
How social internet networking
impacts traveller individual behavior

● Cultural distance on satisfaction
and respect travel intention
    Lifestyle factor influences travel
behavior
● How any why peer-to-peer
accommodation can impact
business tourism pattern
Factors influence local tourists'
destination choice
    Economic environment influence driving
traveller behavior
    What are usually travel behaviors
and attitudes to disabled tourists

How social internet networking
impacts driving traveler behavior

Economic methods measure Consumer shopping behaviors

CHAPTER ONE

The national income GDP measurement consumer behavior

The national income accounting measurement is one good method to help any development countries to research whether what issues are their weaknesses or strengths is order to improve their economic development challenge. The central concept in national accouting is to measure the total output of products or services of the country's economy over a given time period.

The measure is known or gross domestic product (GDP). Output is produced by employing various factors of production (mainly labor and captial), and the revenue from sale of output of used to make payments to these factors of production. The value of output is identified, to the value of income paidout, or what is known as national income. Since the output produced is sold (or added to stocks), the value of output is also equal to the value of expenditure.

Hence, GDP can bre regarded as the value of output produced (appregate supply), the total value of expenditure on output (aggregate demand) or the total value of income in producing the output (real income). So, any developing countries can find whether how much or amout different industries value of output produced from and the real aggregate demand from consumers for different industries' products sale number or services demand in order find whether what factors cause the kind of industry's total GDP product sale number and real income reduction amount. For example, last year, the developing country's cloth industry sale number has 600,000 pieces and real GDP income has US$5 million. But, this year, its cloth industry sale number has 400,000 pieces and real GDP income has US\$ 2 million. Hence, the developing countries can know its current year overall cloth industry sale number and GDP real income must reduce. Then, this country can attempt to find any factors had influenced itself cloth industry why this country itself cloth buyers number and their wearing demand has reduced. the reasons may include overall cloths price is exceed the normal price level or too high to compare its other foreign cloth sellers (overall local cloths price is exceed foreign cloth sellers' price extremely, or overall cloth fashion is not update or not attractive or quality is poor, or import cloth material producing price is too high to cause overall cloth sellers' cloth sale prices are needed to rise in order to earn balance profit or avoid reducing profit, or this developing country's cloth sellers' loyalties or brands are not famous to influence overall local cloth buyers know to choose to buy in itself country. Hence, this developing country can attempt to apply macroeconomic behavioral method to find whether what it/are the main factor(s) to cause its overall cloth industry's real GDP income and sale number is influenced to fall down suddenly in this year.

This macroeconomic country income measurement method can also measure why or what factors cause its any industries' overall supply and demand imbalance problem existence or cause. The reader will notice that the aggregate supply curve (AS) is drawn with an upward slope from left or right. So that at higher price levels more output is provided obviously, there will be a point when, given fixed amount of captial, labor and technology, output can not be increased in the short term.

This represents the full employment level, and at this point, the aggregrate suply curve will become vertical. The aggregate demand cuve simply shows the relationship between the total amount of products and services consumers desire and the price level. For one developing country's overall computer industry example, if it had overall aggregate supply of computer manufacturing number is one million pieces last year, but this year, it's aggregate supply of computer supply of computer manufacturing number is only five hundred thousand pieces. Hence, its overall computer aggregate manufacturing number fell down half pieces in this year.

But if it's overall computer buyers aggregate demand number climbed up from last year one million number to two million number this year. It means that this developing country has overall computer manufacturing number shortage problem to amy local computer sellers in this year. Why does it encounter computer manufacturing number shortage problem? The reasons may include: lacking high technological material supplies to manufacture any laptops or desktops for itself country's computer manufacturers, lacking technician labors to manufacture computers , it is possible due to many technicians choose to go to overseas to seek new computer manufacturing jobs, because they feel salaries are low or poor welfare from local computer employers, or computer manufacturers number decreases or close their businesses number increase, dismissing many computer technician labors , they are replaced by artifical intelligence or manufacturing machines, which are used to manufacture any computer products, or the country's overall computer manufacturing technology is not advanced to adapt to manufacture nowadays computer products.

On conclusion, any developing countries can apply national income measurement method to attempt to find what factor(s) cause(S) its aggregate supply and demand imbalance problem existence. Hence, national income measurement method is one kind of good macroeconomic behavioral method to measure or find why what reasons cause its some industries' products supply and demand number is imbalance or sale number and real GDP income decreases suddenly. Hence, any developing countries can apply macroeconomic analysis to find any factors to cause their any industries' development challenges in possible.

1.1 Industries economic methods

Industries economic theory explains how share the common feature of objectives for the firms (whether profit maximisation, growth of sales maximisation, satisfying etc.) and investigate the consequences of the pursuit of these objectives. Hence, industries economic theory can be attempted to find why the firm's customer number reduces, profir level is felt sudden higher to consumers, why customer's satisfactory level is low to the company's products. Due to the conduct of any firms covers the objectives, price-setting behavior, and attitudes to rivals (actual and potential). For example, if the country's publishing industry's competition rivals are more, due to it permits many overseas publishers enter to itsseld domestic publishing market. So, its local publishers will feel more pressure to attract its readers to choose its local any publishers' books to buy because they have different countries' publishers choices to buy any books in their country.

Hence, the country's local publishing industry structural features of perfect different countries; publishers' competitions are a large number of overseas publishing firms of roughly equal size with free entry into this country's publishing industry suddenly. Even, this country's publishing industry book sellers does not plan to reduce their books sales prices or their books sale prices are not higher to compare their any one overseas publishers' books sale prices.

I believe that this country's local publishing firms readers number can not increase easy immediately because it is not the main reason of this country's overall local publishers' books sale prices are higher issue. It is due to its government permits many differen overseas countries' publishers free enter to itself local publishing market raise itself county's overall books sale effort for its local publoshers. So, it is unfaire to this country's local all publishers as well as free entry publishing market structure influences its all publishers' sale performance to improve easily. It ensures that a free entry market structure challenge to cause this country's publishers feel book sale difficult challenge.

The another case is that when many firms are grouped together as an industry and as firms which seell in the same market, e.g. perfect competition, homogenous, oligopoly and monopoly. In these causes, an industry's defined in terms of a product and the products of that product are members of the industry. Market and industry are very closely related in the case of homogenous products. It is assumed that each firm produces only one of a particular form to a specific industry in terms. If the nature of the firm's output and product which defined the industry.

What happens when a world of differentiated products and of multiproduct firms is considered? the existence of differentiated products can avoid these products which are close substitutes in demand. More formaly, a group of products (or services) is considered as close substitutes for each other when the cross or services is greater than some others. For example, if the country's computer industry has many similar laptop or desktop computer products are selling in itself country. When each groupinf the country's any computer brands products are close substitutes, but between any two kinds either desktop or laptop computer products in different computer brands grouping , the degree of substitution is low.

In this approach, the country's computer industry is defined in terms of high demand conditions to any brands of commputer firms in this country and it would be expected that the size of this country's computer industry would depend on the degree of substitutability used. Hence, it implies this country;s computer industry is very suitable to produce a homegeneous computer product under similar or identical cost conditions, due to itself country's computer buyers won't easy to change their computer purchase choices, when they feel another brand computer firm (later another brand computer product choice) which can provide the similar computer brand product feature or function to replace their the early or prior computer brand product choice easily.

Applied more economic method solves
consumer behavioral challenge

Can apply macro economic method to predict consumer variable behavior to any country? For example, when and how and why do the country consumers , they reduce shopping times or consumption desires in the country. For production and the labor market concept, production is integrated into the general equilibrium framework by firms. Firms utilize capital and labor to produce output and maximize the wealth of the agents who own them.

Households (house consumers) now maximize their utility through the consumption of commodities and leisure in themselves country. Households provide labor inputs to firms in return for wages in order to be able to obtain commodities. There are now markets for factor of production , capital and labor, in addition to commodity market.

In short run, the marginal product of labor (the extra amount of output obtained by adding another unit of labor) fulls as a firm takes on more employees. Profit-maximizing firms will increase employment to the level at which the revenue resulting from employment an additional employee equals the marginal cost of an extra employee. Thus, the lower the real wage, the higher the demand for labor. Individual workers maximize utility by choosing the optimium combinations of work and leisure and the supply of labor's defined as the level of employment forthcoming at a given real wage rate.

Hence, all who desire to find employment at the existing level of real wages will do so , when the country's employment condition and product sale number both are in equilibrium , due to the country's businessmen must have enough buyers number as well as their demands are still increasing. Then , the country's employers will choose to increase employees number or increase wage to attract them to help their businesses to increase more productivities.

So, it explains when on developing country has high unemployment ratio to compare other general developing countries . It implies that itself country's consumers' shopping desires will reduce or their shopping times will reduce, because their shopping desires reduce,, it influences the country's businessmens' products sale number will also reduce. Then, they will choose to reduce employees number or reduce their wages to compensate their sale loss in possible.

On conclusion, in macro economic view, it proves that it has direct or indirect case and effect relationship between the country itself employment rate and the year consumers overall shopping times or consumption desires level and overall market GDP (consumer expenditure overall amount in the year. It can apply the year employment rate number to measure whether the country's consumer shopping desires had been reducing or had been raising in the country in possible. Hence, any country's difference between the year employment ratio and last yeaar employment ratio which can explain why it's the year overall consumption market GDP amount had risen up or has fallen down in possible in order to predict what reasons cause this country's consumer shopping desires to be increase or decrease.

Behavioral economy consumption
desires measurement method

How to apply behavioral economic theory to measure consumption level or consumption desire to the country? I shall assume that consumption is to be measured by private and public expenditures at constant prices at conventionally defined and all money prices are assumed constant. How to measure real consumption?

In fact, consumer behavior has relationship to any country, itself economic growth or recesion in any economic and consumption environment . The purpose of income calculations in practiced affairs to give consumers an indication of the amount which they can consume. It would seem that we ought to define a man's income as the maximum value, which he can consume during a week, and still expect to be well at the end of week as he has at the beginning.

An economy which uses money , but uses it is as a neutral link between transactions in real things and real assets and does not want of a better , a real exchange economy with an economy in which money plays a part of its own and affects motives and decisions and as , in short, one of the operative factors in the situation. So that the course of events can not be predicted either in the long period or in the short period, without knowledge of the behavior of money between the first state and last. It is a monetary economy means to influence any country itself consumer behavioral consumption desires change to more or less shopping times.

Hence, money matters in both the long and short run. Money affects real decision making and employment and output outcomes to any countries. The economic system is moving through calendar time from an irrevocable past to an uncertain and statistically unpredictable future.

Any country's past and present consumption market data do not necessary provide correct signals regarding future outcomes. Ths means that economic data are not necessarily generated by a process. Constrasts denominated in money terms are a human in an entrepreneurial economy. It helps humans efficiently organize time-consuming production and exchange processes in a world of uncertainty.

In any money using entreprensurial economy, entrepreneurs' decisions regarding production and hiring depend on expectations of receiving contractual sales revenues (cash inflows) in excess of the contractual money costs of production (cash outflows). Since, the money wage contract is the most efficient oriented contracts, modern economies can be characterized as money-wage contract-based systems.

Hence, money processes two essential elasticity that differentiate is from the products of industry. These describe why (a) money does not grow on trees (money's elasticity of production is zero)and (b) why producible products are not good liquid stores of value (the elasticity of substitution between liquid assets , such as money and producible products is zero).

If money has these elasticity , then unemployment develops, that is to say, because people can not be employed, when the object of desire (i.e. money, good useful product or good quality product , even shopping enjoyable feeling,) is something which can not produced and the demand of shopping desires are reduced to the country's people.

Hence, unemployment rather than full employment is a normal outcome in any entrepreneurial, market oriented, money-contract-using system in a free competition market environment to the country. So, when the country's people consumption desires are reduced in possible , because unemployment rare rises or living of cost rises, general products prices rise, a spot or commodity price inflation etc. different factors. Then, they will influence the country's economic recession occurrence more easily.

Thus, any countries leaders can not neglect the relationship between unemployment and consumption desire and economic growth or recession relationship. Because in long term, unemployment ratio rises, it has possible to bring many consumers their shopping desires to be reduced as well as economic recession effect to the country.

It implies that any countries' consumers desires, which has relationship to whether themselves jobs supplying number is enough to let themselves countries' people to work. However, labor shortage issue must be better to compare job supplying shortage issue to any country, because labor shortage won't influence consumers' shopping desires to be reduced absolute. It will influence any businesses' productivities are less or reaching the low productive level. Otherwise, jobs supplying shortage will influence consumers' shopping desires to be reduced in the country. It is possible due to the country has many people lose their jobs suddenly. Then, they can not accept to spend money to buy too much any things in their countries easily. On conclusion, any countries' consumer behaviors or consumption desires must have relationship to themselves countries' jobs supplying number. Hence, any countries leaders need to concern whether themselves countries have enough jobs supply to let low education or high education people to work in order to satisfy their living needs in nowadays societies.

CHAPTER TWO

War environment influences consumer behavior

Can wars impact global economy threat?

How did First World War influence Europe economy ?

Can wars bring either advantages or disadvantages or both to impact our economy growth ?In history, I feel that international war can influence any country's economy development has either positive or negative impact in possible.

On the inflationary hand, for the First World War economy growth influence example, in the First World War and since most notably the German hyperinflation of the 1920 year, this type of monetary regime shows a far smaller tendency towards inflation. In the First World War period, volatility of inflation and output were higher in the short run. So, First World War had little negative impact to influence world inflation in the war period. However, in the First World War period, the supply of money was determined not by the rates of economic growth only, but by the amount of available gold and could not be adjusted in response to economic needs. So, new sources of gold would increase money supply and inflation and decrease interest rates , the opposite of what modern central banks would do to provide stable economic growth in First World War. So, it explained that the First World War occurrence caused the change from non-inflationary to inflationary long term development. Thus, it seems First World War brings more money supply and gold supply to stable economic growth in the future long term period.

On the labor productivity influence hand, leaving monetary issues aside, the First World War created the working time intellectual mood to change labor productivity, it would be a 15-18 hours working week for more enlightened leisure to Europe labors. Some prominent modern economists on the accuracy of the predictions on GDP growth per capital was remarkably accurate given to be fallen down that it was made at the time when economy growth theory did not even exist in the First World War period. Thus, it seems First World War also causes working time to be raised to the developing countries during the industrialization period. Then, the long time working time brought to the developing countries' workers to it is poor for labor health. Hence, although employers can raise productivity, but they need many workers to work long time to cause unhealthy. The majority found that the prediction on leisure is of the variations between world regions , due to income level exist, making European variety of capitalism. So, the First World War caused income inequality within countries and between nation states, trends in working hours , world poverty and ever growing needs (consumerism) and the like. Thus, the developed western countries' workers can work lesser time to compare to the developing Asia countries' workers. Consequently, First World War brought negative impact to influence the developing Asia countries' worker unhealthy and physical and mental illnesses number had been increasing as well as it brought positive impact to influence the labor productivity had been increasing to the Asia countries' employers, due to their workers need to work long time every day.

It seems on the positive impact hand, that the First World War caused the inflation occurrence to bring more money supply and gold supply to be raised to influence global economic growth. But, on the negative impact hand, it also brought low working hours in European developed countries and high working hours to the Asia developing countries which are needed to do different occupations in developing countries as well as the income inequality caused unfair social challenge had also occurred in developed countries, such as Europe, UK, US etc. and developing countries, such as China, Japan, Korea etc . Thus, First World War had brought developed countries better economy development and better salary and less working hours to labors because Europe had reached the mature stage of industrialization to avoid labors who needed to work overtime. Otherwise, it had brought developing countries poor economy development and poor salary and labors need work long time to raise productivities.

In conclusion, it implied that the First World War had bought some bad influences to developing countries' economic system, e.g. social income inequality, working hours inequality, inflation and GDP per capita going down in the past Europe economic history development, but it also bought welfares to developed countries' European labor working time intellectual mood to change labor productivity, it would be a 15-18 hours working week for more enlightened leisure to Europe labors. So, it seemed to cause negative economic influence to developing countries, but it cause positive economic influence to developed counties during the First World War time.

● Are US poor economic consequences of war?

What are the macroeconomic effects of US government spending on the war? I believe modern times are that the human cost military spending has created positive economic outcomes for the US economy. I shall indicate how the human costs of war influences positive economic outcomes for the US on these aspects which include: GDP, consumption , investment , inflation and income distribution aspects.

In fact, US heightened military spending can create employment additional economic activity and contributes to the military weapon development of new technologies, which can bring advantages into other industries in US. For long term economic influence, US military weapon research and development on creating employment would potentially have the same low cost economic benefit in US. For example, US economy had higher GDP growth in the Afghanistan and Iraq war period. Another benefit is that US had appropriate conditions for future growth after the Second World War great depression period. It was a sharp decline in income inequality and the trend in declining inequality standard after the Second World War great depression period. Thus, America's human cost military spending could bring indirect military weapon research and development on creating employment benefit and it would potentially have the same low cost economic benefit in US. However, in the war period, the higher levels of government military weapon spending with war tends to generate some positive economic benefits in the short-term period, specifically through increases in economic growth during spending booms after war period.

Why it can bring GDP growth in the US war period. In general, by the end of World Ward II, US GDP was over 120 % and tax revenue increased more than three times to over 20% of GDP. However, GDP growth there was are increase in the trend lines after the war had finished when unemployment was eliminated, recovery was well underway prior to the war, are the key counterfactual is whether similar spending on US public works would have generated even more growth. However, US macroeconomic history over the past seventy years, that there are a number of negative economic effects from conducting any wars. But, there have also positive benefits of increases US government spending on military industry. Moreover, when an economy has excess capacity and unemployment , it is possible that increasing military spending can provide an important stimulus. When military and defense spending is important in providing security for the US nation as well as helping to support and protect US's national affect.

So, in war economic view point, it will bring this question: Is efficiency or justification for any particular macroeconomic effects of war spending for US? To answer this question, I shall suppose security is not only dependent on an adequate military capability , but security can also keep on economic stability. For example, price controls strategy and rationing strategy had a significant role to play to influence consumption in US, during war period. For example, it was difficult for household to purchase products , such as washing machines, irons or water heaters because the raw resources, e.g. steel and production capabilities are needed to be used to produce military weapons instead of these products effort to prepare to fight the enemy in the Second World War. So, the raw resources, e.g. steel price will be rasied, due to shortage to supply to produce the home consumer products , Then, it will bring the home consumer products price to be raised. So, war will bring negative impact to influence home consumer product prices to be raised, due to shortage of steel resources supply when they are supplied to produce weapon to win enemy in war period. Consequently, In war period negative resource shortge hand, as the same time, the war production board was able to assign priorities to scare materials, such as rubber, steel and aluminum to ensure which went to production of the military, rather than to civilian products. In addition, wages were controlled and personal savings were encouraged through the purchase of war bonds which further limited the size of individual's disposable income during the Second World War period.

Moreover, in the war period, it also bring food price raising, due to food supply shortage and poor living standrd to poor people, even rich people. Due to people were also encouraged to conserve food and produce as much of that own food as possible because food items were generally scare. Freezes were also stayed for wages. Combined with a general reduction in consumption, it can be said living standards for whose already employed, at least in material terms did not improved , even to rich people.

It means that war will influence people quality of life to be fallen down. Even, in terms of total GDP. Such as World War II (WWII) did not create a permanent increase or change in the growth the trend after the war had ended. However, the positive lasting effort for WWII was a more even distribution of wealth. This reallocation of income created the ideal conditions for the formation of an advancement consumer economy till to nowadays.

However, on war long time influence hand, the WWII influenced US economy to be changed to be better, such as material well being was affected by tax increases, new price and wage controls which constrained private sector consumption and investment is encouraged, due to World War II had destroyed the traditional material development, so it also encouraged new investors to invest to any Asia or Europea new businesses.

● Can war economy policy influence peace and security?

I believe war economics policy may contribute to international peace and security as positive impact more than negative impact. The reasons are as below:

A first positive attitude behavioral possibility , any war economic policy can increase international interdependence through trade and finance raises the potential costs of war to a degree that makes welfare an irrational option of foreign policy can raise economic growth and builds good trading relationship between countries. Moreover, the use of superior economic and military power to harm an actual or potential aggressor's economy and make it stops preparing of waging war, e.g. US restricted Mexico imported to itself country, US invented military weapons to threaten to Korea to avoid nuclear war occurrence. In the past, US spent to military expenditure which could rise to employ soldier numbers to reduce unemployment as well as assisted military weapon manufacturers needed to employ many manufacturing workers to manufacture many military weapons for US government military fighting need.

Hence, the relationship between war and economy will bring this basic question: Whether either can economics provide a growing tool for avoiding war or whether may consumption for resources and markets result in an increased likelihood of war? Following the increase of international trade and financial transfers in modern times. However, there has been a growing to concern the economic wisdom of war.

Liberal economists oppose the idea that war might be a good business and advocated the promotion of peace and advocated the promotion of peace by international economic links among the different countries. Although, history has shown that enlightened economic self-interest was not always alike to contribute to the ultimate avoidance of war. But, a short overview of the liberal peace theory indicates, it takes a look at the amount ability of economic instruments as a means to enforce peace by an economically superior country or group of countries, e.g. within the framework of the United Nations or of regional organization for security and cooperation in Europe, the African Union or the organization of American States.

How civil wars influence positive or negative impact?

On country itself civil war negative impact hand, what is the impact of civil wars on economic growth at domestic and in nearby countries? Some economists believe civil war can have a profound negative influence on the economic fortunes of a country or its neighbors, e.g. owing to a loss of human capital, a destruction of infrastructure and reductions in investment and trade and daily market activities. Within the period of measurement have economic consequences , the economists scale the civil war variable to be better identify their relative impacts. They indicate the distance between countries which is a factor provides the most accurate measure of the negative economic consequences of civil wars on other countries.

On country itself civil war positive impact hand, in economic view point, the country itself civil war indicates the income and capital input terms. Since, everything is in per capita terms. Due to civil war encourage technological development. Technology changes are in the investment in labor effectiveness. The capital includes physical and human capital . How civil war influences efficiency growth . The growth in labor's enhanced efficiency is from technology change and capital depreciation. So, anything that can raise labor growth or its improved efficiency, increases the denominator or capital per capita and so reduced its growth and that of incomer per capita. Depreciation or the gradual wearing down of capita; through use or age also limits capital growth. Some economists suggest that war migration is a good growth of labor to influence the immigration country's economic growth. For example, the inflow of refugees from a nearby civil war can lead to in-migration and adversely affect income per capita growth. Migration may , however, influences the in-migration country economic growth if the migrants bring in human capital, due to civil war.

Consequently, from a theoretical perspective, civil wars can adversely affect income per capita growth at home through a number of avenues. So civil war will cause bad influence to home country, the reasons are as below:

The reasons include:

First, a civil conflict can destroy physical and human capital. Second, by the international trade flows, and day-to-day marketing activities, civil wars can inhibit growth. Third, civil wars may divert the inflow of foreign direct investment (FDI) owing to heightened perceived risks of investors. Because (FDI) perceived is an imported source of savings that finances investment. So, a fill in FDI results in reduced growth. Heightened instability and risks will also limit investment at home and cause a flight of savings abroad. Fourth, civil wars cause indirect government defense expenditures from productive social overhead capital e.g. roads, public schools and bridges, gardens to less productive defense spending. Fifth, such wars may cause the internal displacement of people as their homes either come under serious control or are destroyed. So that income per capita is adversely influenced. Sixth, civil wars often result in the breakdown of the health lead to lack of medical care, less clean drinking water and reduced sanitation , all of which have negative consequences on economic activities and growth .

Thus, any country itelf civil war can bring negative impacts more than positive impacts. Due to economic impacts may even increase further from some conflicts as nearby countries reduce trade with others in the regions and potential investors brand , even non-neighboring countries have as poor investment risks. Thus, there are four potential channels , such as human capital, physical capital, labor growth and an intercept shift are influenced by civil wars as well as which can influence income per capita growth in other nearby countries. To conclude, neighboring countries need to concern how to avoid civil war is caused to occur among themselves because civil wars will have negative impact to influence their economic growth.

● How economic positive and negative impact of the war to higher military spending?

Most models show that military spending to divert resources from productive uses, such as consumption and investment , and ultimately slows economic growth and reduces employment. So, it seems war causes disadvantages more than advantages to influence economy growth to any countries in possible.

Some economists showed global insight produced a set of projections that compared a scenario with an increase in annual military spending equal to 1.0% of GDP current about $135billions relative to its baseline scenario . This is approximately equal to the increase in defense spending that has taken place compared with the pre-Sept. 11th terrorism Iraq war baseline to US government higher military spending. However, who also indicated military spending is not generally perceived to cost jobs.

In standard economic models, war its positive impact can be thought of in the same way as spending on the environment from war bad influence. When tax and emission restrictions are often used to achieve environment protection during and after war. It is also possible to reach environmental targets by paying people to do things that will reduce pollution. For example, it is possible to reduce greenhouse gas emissions by paying people to buy more fuel efficient cars and appliances, or paying than to install insulation and other energy saving devices. So, during the war period, more greenhouse gas fuel efficient cars will increase demand in car market. Thus, war can reduce air and water pollution cost and encourage greenhouse gas fuel consumption. In the case of both increased military spending and paying people to take steps to reduce greenhouse gas emissions, resources would be reduced to supply to these countries' domestic market directed uses.

In standard economic models, war it's negative impact to this redirection of other resources, due to the original resources are used to increase military spending to manufacturing any new weapons and it will cause this original resources are shortage to prepare for these countries' manufacturing countries. So, these resources shortage challenges will cause these military spending countries' economy to operate less efficiently and therefore lead to slower growth and fewer jobs supplies. Thus, war will bring resource shortage challenges and fewer jobs supplies bad influence. In policy debates, it is important to recognize the potential jobs losses are caused from military spending factor mainly. Also the potential economic costs are often a factor in debates over environment policy.

Due to war causes the military countries' air and water pollution challenges. So, the military countries' wars occurrence will raise the water and air pollution cost of chance. It is often believed environmental pollution challenge has relationship between wars and increases in military spending.

So, in this way, any country is carrying on military spending is comparable in most models to any other form of any country's spending, such as spending on public products or improving the environment pollution expenditures. Thus, it seems war will bring environment pollution economic cost more than environment protection economic benefit to any military expending countries.

Country internal civil war influences consumer behavior

The relationship between country itself internal civil war and human welfare

How internal civil war influences human welfare?

Nowadays, a growing number of economists and political scientists often ask this simple question: Why there is so much civil wars in any country itself the world? Poverty is commonly held to be a leading cause of internal wars. Indeed, it has close relationship between low per capita incomes and higher propensities for internal war's countries. Such as developing country Africa, it has many times more internal wars. So, it brings poverty and low living standards and poor health and poor air and water pollution environment to let African to live. Then, hunger and disease will also be caused easily in Africa.

However, internal civil wars also bring negative influences to developed countries, such as Australia, US Canada, UK , Japan, Korea etc. countries. The reason is because the internal civil war counties which refugee flows will choose to immigrate to those developed countries. Such as developing countries, South Korea and Africa and India , there have many times more internal civil wars .So it brings poverty and low living standards and poor health and poor environment to let African , South Korean, Indian to choose to live to these developed countries. Then, hunger and disease will be caused easily in developing and developed both countries, due to developed countries permit these developing countries' refugee who immigrate to themselves countries to live from internal civil war counties refugee immigration easily.

Moreover, internal civil war can also influence developed countries, such as Australia, US, Canada , UK refugee flows will choose to immigrate to these developed countries lawlessness as well as the illicit trades in drugs , arms and minerals will appear into these developed countries neighboring conflict zones . The destructive consequences of internal civil welfare may be a great as to potentially be a factor in the growing gap between the world's richest and poorest nations.

Can internal civil wars influence the country's long run economic development?

Has it relationship between long run economic growth and internal civil war? Some economists recommend that it focuses on impacts on capital and population, the basic of economic production and whether the internal civil war country is possible rapid recovery as well as the internal civil wars cause economic impacts which can also been found for human capital, including measures of education, nutrition, health and productivity to the internal civil war countries.

What are intenal civil war negative impacts? Some behavior economists had experimented one interesting research to indicate that any internal civil war country will reduce human resource productivity growth , will reduce overall GDP in possible. Their research indicated the internal war armed group leaders are most motivate citizens to be soldiers for their side. Participation becomes easier to motivate the lower is citizen's opportunity cost of fighting . So there models predict that the amount of citizens' time devoted to fighting increases as the returns to fighting rise relative to the returns to reduce human resources supply to society to assist enterprises to raise any productive activities.

Consequently, in economic view point, if the internal civil war countries citizen will be trained to be soldiers. Then, it will reduce citizen to do other occupations in the internal war period. Also, the internal civil war countries will reduce their citizen have time and effort to do other social occupations to assist countries' economy development in the internal civil war period. Moreover, the internal civil war countries citizen, such as human resource number will be shortage to supply to satisfy their countries' enterprises' needs in the internal civil war period. It will influence economic growth to be go down during the internal civil war period to the internal civil war countries for either short term or long term. Even, the natural resource supply, e.g. water, food, vehicle gas etc. will be concentrate on spending to satisfy the soldiers' needs. It will cause natural resource shortage to supply to satisfy to citizen's life needs daily in the natural civil war period. So, the internal civil war will bring disadvantage to influence economic growth to the internal civil war countries.

How can reduce the risks of the civil internal war to influence economy growth?

How can reduce the risks when internal civil war occurs in the country? What factors explain variations in the duration of civil internal wars, and why should policymakers care? I shall suppose to the duration of civil internal wars , which should be implicated in their destructiveness to the civil internal war country as well as long time duration of civil internal wars should have long time poor economic influence to the civil internal war country.

At any given point in a civil internal war, the civil internal war country government (A) and the civil internal war country rebels(B) each must choose between stopping or continuing to flight.

This implies four possible outcomes from their joint decisions at any time.

The first outcome is that if (B) continues flight and (A) stops, (B) wins and the government (A) is overthrown.

The second outcome is that if government (A) flights and (B) stops, (A) wins and the revolt is defeated (B) .

The third outcome is that if both (A) and (B) choose to stop flight at the same time, the civil internal war ends to be a negotiated settlement.

The fourth outcome is that if neither decides to stop, the civil internal war continues (Stam 1996 , 34-37).

Stam (1996, 353) again indicated the four outcomes can be represented as an two person game. Continued flight is the dominant strategy for both sides.

Thus, it seems negotiated settlement is the best solution to solve any civil internal war because it won't have either win or loss outcome to either of party, it will have win outcome to both countries.

In economic welfare view point, they will discuss how to earn the much economic benefits to achieve the reasonable negotiation fairly. It is a two parties win-to-win method to both supported government and not supported government parties both. Because usually the cause of any internal civil war , due to the not supported (disagreed) government party feel whose government is unfair to give reasonable and fair much economic welfare to them in society. So, they (part of citizen) only choose to cause internal civil war to let their country to know that who feel dissatisfactory at the time.

In economic view point, unfair resource allocation challenge will cause any internal civil war easily in any country. Thus, it means that any country government ought to know when and how to allocate its limited resources to let its citizen to feel fair to use (spend) in society when resources are not shortage to supply to them to consume. Also, it means how to allocate (spend) limited resource to prepare any countries' citizen to enjoy to consume. So, it is one important question to any country government to concern if which wanted to reduce internal civil war occurrence chance on nowadays societies. Thus, it seems that any country itself internal civil war will bring disadvantages more than advantages.

Bibliography

Stam , A. C. 1996, Win, Lose or Draw: Domestic politics and the crucible of war . Ann Arbor: University of Michigan Press.

CHAPTER THREE

Inflation influences consumer behavior

Any countries have chance to encounter inflation problem. Inflation means as a factor that could reduce the saving ration. If consumers expected prices to rise, they would bring forward consumption to take advantage of lower prices. For example, during the 1970s , as both inflation and the saving ration rose theories were advanced to explain why inflation could lead to an increase in saving.

The most clear or reasonable explanation is that households do not base their consumption decisions about consumption and saving on their money income alone consumption and saving on their money income alone, due to they reduce some capital losses from their income. In particular, they reduce some reduction in the real value of monetary assets caused by inflation. So, inflation could affect the savings ratio, due to gains and losses on loans between households cancel out. It depends on where some households deposit money with banks.

How can consumption function explain it has relationship between the savings ratio and inflation have been suggested by some economists ? The reasons may include as below:

(1) There may be a link between changes in income and changes in consumption. If consumption during a quarter is related to money income in the previous quarter, then a acceleration (accumulation) in wages and prices will lead to a fall in real consumption in the quarter following the accumulation, and in a rise in the savings ratio. So, it explains why money incomes and savings will have risen , but real consumption will long fallen. Because the inflation influences the incomes and savings seem rise, but in fact, if the consumption amouts and numbers do not rise when the inflation period. The country's consumers' whose shopping desires or real

consumptions do not real rise as the same time in the period. Unless, the country's general consumers can accept to spend much expenditure to buy more number of any things in themselves societies. Otherwisem, the real consumption effect will not be achieved in the country.

(2) The uncertainty created by a high and unstable rate of inflation could cause people to save more. The degree of uncertainty is difficult to quantify and may not be tied to the inflation rate in a simple linear relationship. So, due to any countries' citizen or consumers or living people who must not predict when inflation will come. Because this uncertain when inflation occurrence reason, many consumers will not change their habit consumption behaviors, such as habitly spending much consumers, they won't change their consumption habits to be reduced number or consumption times easily or habitly spending less consumers, they won't change their consumption habits to be raised number or consumption times easily. Even, they predict inflation will come as soon. Because inflation predicting feeling will be more uncertain to influence their spending behaviors changing more easily. Unless the country's government can ensure to notice its citizen when inflation will come, then it will influence their shopping times or consumption number to be changed easily.

(3) The personal factor includes businesses, and stock or share investment appreciation during periods of inflation may boost savings. So, the county will have many citizen choose to save more money to bank if they feel inflation will come as soon in possible. They won't like to spend much expenditure to buy any things easily because they will feel unreasonable price or unfair purchase and sale transaction in social market in the moment.

(4) Unexpected inflation favours bank borrowers (bank debtors) and bank itself (bank creditors) both roles. So, it tends to favour the young who borrow to buy houses, or much entertainment consumption enjoyment spending when they feel inflation will occur to influence house price to be rised or any things and entertainment expenditures to be rised also. Because if banks informed inflation will be occur in possible soon, this prediction will let the feeling long term living house needed buyers whom will choose to borrow much money in order to buy any houses in the short time. They aim to avoid inflation causes general houses price to be risen and bringing unreasonable and unfair house purchase prices when inflation is real occurred soon. Thus, the bank creditors marginal propensity to same could be lower that of debtors (bank borrowers).

I believe that it has close relationship between income saving ratio and inflation and consumption desire. Such as the economist keynes's (1981) hypothesis assumes that some degree supported by the proportion of income saved increased as income ought rise or the same live in general countries' consumption condition or economic environment. He indicated that , for example, there are other explanation for the rising British savings ratio during 1960 s. His opinions were based on below evidences:

(1) The low savings ratio cria 1950 s was a reaction to shortage of products and forced saving during war time and the early post war period. When many types of products were not variable to buy or were rationed. The rising savings ratio during the 1950 s probably contained an accurate prediction of recovery a normal level.

(2) There were demographic and social changes factors in UK in between 1950s and 1960s. The principle change was the spread of pension funds. This increased the level of committed saving as the proportion of the UK population who were members of pension schemes increased, though a part of saving through pension schemes may be offset by a reduction in other forms of saving, e.g. net saving through life insurance schemes increased from 5.7 % of PDI between 1960s and 1981 year.

So, changes in UK population structure in this period are another factor influencing the savings ratio. Children are expensive any may cause a fall in income as well, consumption function in the direction of increased saving. Any increase in the UK proportion of married women in the UK working population could have increased the saving ratio. On the other side, the increasing proportion of the UK elderly in the UK population probably reduce it. On conclusion, the influence saving ratio raising factors to the country UK which may include: raising the country's population beween 1960s to 1981s which may include: the children and elderly number increase or decrease, pension and insurance product saving plan, lacking enough variable kinds of products choice to let consumers buy after war period main factors and inflation main factors. So, it impact consumer shopping desire will fall down to UK in the after war period between 1960s. and 1981s.

On conclusion, if the country hope to raise consumer desire, the methods may include that banks discourage saving interest reducing or stable staying plan and insurance plans promotion, inflation will come soon information, young population immigration number increases, creating many jobs to low and high education people to work, exciting employers raise salary, encouraging rent houses choice to house buyers. However, macro economic-inflation consumption and the savings ratio can be the best method to predict whether consumer desire will rise up or fall down to the country because if the country has many people have already saved money to bank, it implies that many people do not like to buy any things, due to they feel inflation will come soon. Otherwise, when if the country has less people decide to save money to bank, it implies that many people like to buy any things, due to they feel inflation will not come soon. So, it ought have close relationship between the saving ratio and inflation and consumption desire to any countries.

Source: Economic trends, Nov. 1981, p.16

Micro or macro economic method

consumer desire measurement

The role of economy can measure consumer behavior, it can be used to analyze and gather social data, e.g. how many different brands of product are selling in the country, how many youth people, working people, old peole age groups are living in the country, how many the kind of product number is sold in the yar, how many average shopping times to the kind product to the country overall consumers number in the year, how long useful time to be replaced another new product , the counry's consumers they use the kind of product. Consequently, economist can conclude the effect of the kind of product sale number, different age of consumers' purchase times and useful time etc. different market data in order to predict whether the kind of product ought be manufactured how many number which is the most suitable number as well as whether the reasonable price level is to achieve the most highest sale income to the country's the kind of brand product next year.

In general, consumer behavioral research economists have improved the research task of analysing and predicting econmic change how it can influence consumer behavior. A great deal of econometic work has been devoted to building and testing models, that is systems of relationships designed to how the interdependent variation of a set of variable, and with estimating the constants in these consumer behavioral inlfuence models.

Moreover, a system of equations in which the values of some variables appear for consecutive time periods can be used for any countries' consumer behavioral changing prediction purposes , but the predictions which can be dervied express the way in which the system would vary through time if it were allowed to run undistributed. Ths aspect ot the research consumer behavioral changing matter is now recognized and specifies the assumed properties , since they have importance bearing not only in prediction, but also on the estimation, e.g. how and why and when the country's consumer purchase habit will sudden change. Hence, the consumer behavioral research economists' role is to provide the country's market information about the systematic factors at work , so that the variable element of guess-work is reduced as far as possible.

All practical economists who are not econometricians will readily assent to this statement as it relates to identities or definitions. No one in his senses will be content with predictions: what the most minimum of income level influences consumer individual shopping desire reduces, what the most minimum of savings level influences general consumers' shopping desires reduce etc. which do not satisfy the usual accounting identifies.

Economics is the science which indicates human (consumer) role is as a relationship between (achieving sale effect) and consumers feel scarce to buy the product (psychological response), because general consumers feel scarce or shortage supplying to the product in themselves coutry market. They will choose to attempt to visit any shops to buy the product immediately. So, scarce or shortage supplying factor may be one important factor to influence general consumers expect to buy the kind of product immediately if they feel the brand of product is shortage to sell to them in any shops in the country. It may be more important to compare cheaper price factor, inflation factor, the shop's geographical location far away to the consumer individual home factor, savings or investment etc. different factors to influence the country's consumers purchase desires to be rised up or fallen down.

The economc methods measure consumer behaviors (purpose to accept primary facts. Hence is on the quantitative side a further type of information. By primary facts, I mean such things as the originating entries in a firm's sale cash book or the quantity of some commodity produced over a particular period. On the other hand, there are many items, similar to primary facts in the actual world, but which are not capable of being in the same simple manner, e.g. the income of an individual or a nation GDP. These data is the best consumer behavioral changing to the country's social consumption market.

The principle problems which the answering of questions of fact sets to the economic statisticans can conveniently be analyzed in the familiar terms of demand and supply concerns to research how, why and when the kind of product's consumer shopping desires whether they will like to choose either buy more or less to the kind of product. We first have to decide what we want to know and then consider how we are going to find it out.

For the point of view of the user of factual information. The obvious approach to the research how, why and when consumer shopping desires change to the kind of product purchase choice issue. A system for ascertaining facts which worked on this principle, such as how many economic facts are ascertained to the country's consumption market concerns to the kind of product. There is no point in trying to ascertain the national income on some given definition to the nearest pounds or UK dollar measured when in fact no use for the information could be concerned that required it to be accurate to more than the nearest 10 million pound or UK dollar for England, UK GDP (Gross Domestic Product) income in the year. Hence, GDP is not the most suitable data gathering method to be used to analyze why , how and when consumers behavioral change to the kind of product sale in the country. Because ir is one macro economic view, it is not more accurate to compare micro economic view to measure any country's consumer behavior or shopping desire changes , such as individual income level changes,. Otherwise, these micro economic data ,such as firms sale number and sale income changes etc. data they are more suitable to be used in order to measure whether the kind of product's consumption desire will increase or decrease more accurate for the country next year.

On economics, we meet with a number of different kinds of mathematical relationship. Perhaps the simplest is the definitional relationship which certains only variables linked together which certains only variables linked together by the arithmatic. Examples of such relationships are: Income equals consumption plus saving, the sim of saving by each sector of the economy equals the total saving of economy, the quantity of some commodity sold multiplied by average selling price equals the expenditure on the commodity. These equations do not tell use anything about the behavior of economic agents e.g. consumer behavior: they imply indicate the defined relationships between certain terms. When relationships of this kind form part of a system of equations. They may be used to eliminate certain variable from the system and thus reduce the degrees of freedom of the system.

To go back to the example of the definitional relationship " income equals consumption plus saving", we can obviously calculate it means that income minus consumption, whereever saving appears in a system of relationships. Thus, reducing the number of variables and of equation. As ny explanation indicates that why micro economic data, e.g. indivdual income variable level, saving variable level is more accuate to be gathered to use for judgement when, why and how the kind of product general consumers behaviors or shopping desires change to compare macro economic data , e.g. the country's GDP in the country. Because we can not build up a theory of human behavior with the aid of definitional relationship alone, in addition we shall need relationship of age groups, such as a individual or a young age group, working age group, old age group different age consumers or occupation groups, e.g. professional occupation, such as teacher, doctor, lawyer , or low educational level occupation, such as factory worker etc. different age or occupation consumer groups of a consumption behaviouristic or consumer group character telling us something of the way in which the different individuals or consumer groups behavr or indicating the technical relationships which subsist between, say the input of factors of production and the output of product. Example of such relationships are: The familiar demand and supply to the brand product relationships; the relationship connecting saving to the individual income or general young age group income or old age group income or working people income in the society, and the rate of interest to the country's bank system; a relationship indicating the presence or absence of price control to gas issue concerns how to influence car buyers' purchase cars demands or driving desires. All of these any one of micro economic relationship is the influence of as aspect of the consumer behavioral changing or consumer desire changing system highly relevant to general macro economic behavioral change system to the country.

Is these any advantage in operate with structural equations? The answer is " yes" for the following reasons. In the case of relationship expressing behavior these may be expected to ahve the highest possible degree of performance, since they reflect the behavior of only one type of entity in the system, such as sales and price information equations just mentioned, depend for their stability on the constant responses not of one but of two or more types of entity, in the example both buyers (the kind of product consumers or buyers) and sellers (the kind of product sellers). Thus, if we can assume that the buyers' responses , through not the sellers' responses will remain constant over a period, we can express (or forecast) the quantity transacted by using one equation if we adopt the demand equation. Whereas, we shall need to least two if we adopt that sales equation. Thus, in micro economic view, equation method , such as gathering the kind of sale and price their information, it may help the seller measure whether it ought set up how much sale price to the product to let many consumers feel the most reasonable in order to increase its sale number in the country's consumption market.

On conclusion, consumer behavior measurement, micro economic method is more suitable or acceptable to compare macro economic method in any countries' consumption market nowadays.

CHAPTER FOUR

Unemployment influences consumer desires

Why does global macro economic environment become worse, it will bring many countries' unemployment rates raise as well as it can cause crime rate number rises in possible? I believe that they have case and effect relationship. In most countries, unemployment is higher today than it was in the 1960s. Why are these such large variations in unemployment, it brings more crime after 1960s? I shall indicate the reasons as below:

(1) Hiring costs raise unemployment as firms become more anxious to keep the workers they have,which puts upward pressure on wages. So, when the global societies employers feel any costs are increasing after 1960s, e.g. manufacturing cost, rent cost, office and/or office electricity cost , goods transportation cost , even wage cots etc. hen, many employers will choose to dismiss many workers and unemployment rate will be raised. When many workers lose jobs for long time. Social crime number will increase, in special, the low educational and low skillful workers. Their crime mind and crime behaviors will be caused by long term unemployment.

(2) Generous unemployment benefits may make workers more selective in their job search and raise unemployment. IN fact, after 1960s, global macro economic environment had been improving from manufacturing industry to service, than high technological industries development both. It will cause the developing countries, such as Africa, China, Hong Kong, Korea etc., their low education and low skillful workers lose jobs suddenly, due to their manufacturing skills won't be popular needed to employers. For example, old cloth drwssing machines will be replaced from new high technological cloth dressing machines, old car manufacturing factory method will be replaced by high technological artificial intelligent car manufacturing method. When the low manufacturing skillful workers can

not find any manufacturing jobs to match their manufactury skills in their job search process. Then, in long term unemployment situation, the high technolobical development factor will cause the low manufacturing skillful workers have crime or anti-social psychological mind to cause crime behaviors easily.

(3) Mismatch between worker skills and labor demand means that unemployed workers have differenties competing for jobs which will raise the level of unemployment. Similiar , due to global macro economic environment changes, e.g. many high technological skillful workers number increases, but the supply of high technological skillful workers number can not grow rapidly. So, it brings the shortage of high technological skillful labor supply. Otherwise, in global societies , many low technological skillful workers, they do not continue to learn any kinds of high technological knowledge to prepare to find any high technological jobs easily. So, global societies bring the mismatch between worker skills and labor demand. Consequently, it many bring many low technological skillful workers still lose jobs for long time , Then, their crime behaviors will also be influenced to raise in possible.

(4) Lacking a well-functioning education system and active labor market policy could potentialy raise mismatch and unemployed. The reason is easy to understand. For Hong Kong example, HK crime rate is increasing after 1960s. although, HK's manufacturing industry is replaced by monetary, service industries maninly nowadays. HK lacks a well functioning education system to educate the low educational level and low skillful youngers to be trained their skills to prepare to do further high technological development industry. So, HK's social weakness is a lack of high technological jobs well-functioning education system. It can train many youngers to do high technological jobs in active labor market.

Nowadays, HK has many employers need high technolgical workers in active labor market. It will cause many HK high technological businesses can not find any high technological workers easily in HK. Then, they will choose to find overseas high technological workers to replace HK domestic workers, as well as it will cause HK high technological workers' wages to be reduced. Otherwise, overseas high technological workers' wages will be raised . Even longer time , HK many high technological workers will lose jobs, because their skills can be replaced from overseas high technological workers easily. If their demand still need HK employers raise their salaries to compare to overseas high technological workers' salaries . Due to this global macro high technological workers demand increasing factor influences to HK, so China, or other developing high technological job markets. Then, it may cause many developing countries' high technological workers lose thier jobs, due to the developed countries' high technological workers can be replaced to do their job more easy, even their salaries demand is lower to compare to the developing countries high technological workers' salaries demand. So, when the developing countries ' high technological workers feel unfair, they lose jobs, due to overseas developed countries' high technological wotkers are replaced. It will cause that they will choose to do crime behavior in society more easier.

Also, HK's job security legislation is poor to comapre Western countries. For example, US, UK, New Zealand, Australia etc. Western countries. They have good citizen security legislation. All those Western countries' citizen own unemployment assistance, when they lose jobs to do in long time or they unemploy long time. Then, they have authority to need their governments to give unemployment assistance. If they have no any unemployment or they have less unemployment before 60 or 65 retirement age. Then, after 60 or 65 age, their government will still give them money for life assistance per week, till to they die. Otherwise, HK government only have job security legislation to reduce employee individual 5% of salary for MPF (mututary provident fund) and employee's 5 % salary for MPF maximum per month for their retirement benefit. HK government won't give HK citizen money for life assistance after 65 retirement age. If the HK citizen earned less salary before 65 age, then it is not enough to provide social welfare assistance to any HK citizen after they reach 65 age in possible. So, it explains that why some HK old people will do crime behaviors more easily.

Does long-term unemployment cause social problem? There is no question that high unemployment is a major social problem, but zero unemployment is neither feasible nor a desirable object for poicy. In fact, it is natural and acceptable that some workers are unemployed between different jobs. For example, when one waiter is dismisses or unemployed , due to his restaurant employer loses business or another waiter is employed different reasons . Then, he spends more six months to seek the same waiter job, but he still can not find any same job easily. Then, he chooses to learn any similar waiter service skills, e.g. hotel waiter service skill. He needs to spend another six months to lean the new hotel waiter service and attitude knowledge, because restaurant waiter service skil is very diffeent to hotel waiter service skill need. He needs to learn how to serve hotel restaurant clients. Thus, in this year unemployment minimum period, it includes the six months seeling restaurant waiter job period and another six months learning hotel waiter job learing period, this restaurant waiter unemployed worker won;t earn any salary in this year. It means that long-term unemployment period to this career seeker. Also, it is rational for this restaurant waiter unemployed worker not to take the first restaurant waiter job, he can get , but to attempt to learn hotel restaurant waiter service knowledge to wait for a hotel restaurant waiter job employment in possible, where he can use his specific competence and be rewarded for this with a reasonable waiter occupation wage.

If this restaurant unemployed waiter was occasionally unemployed for a few weeks between jobs, this is not necessarily a big social problem. The really serious socal problem occurs when workers are stuck in unemployment for many months or even years, such as this restaurant unemployed waiter case, he has one year unemployment period at least. It includes, the six months without salary restaurant waiter job search period and another six months without hotel restuarant waiter learning period. Moreover, he also need to pay tuition for this hotel restaurant waiter course as well as he also needs to pass the practice and paper test of hotel restaurant waiter course in order to earn this certificate of their hotel restaurant waiter occupation and he can find any hotel restaurant waiter job more easy. However, if he can not pass this course, then he needs to do choice either paying tuition to study this course again or he can attempt to find the same past restaurant waiter job again or he can attempt to learn another new skill to further change his new occupation career. Then , it brings this question : Does long term unemployment cause or influence this restaurant waiter perform crime behavior in society ? I believe that the answer is depended that how long in typical worker will be unemployed. To see what determines the expected duration of unemployment , assume for simplicity that workers who find a job in a particular month start working at the end of that month, so that all workers who become unemployed remain unemployed for least one month. So, the duration of unemployment depends on three factors as well as these three factors can influence any unemployed workers choose to do crime behaviors in society more easily. They include as below:

(1) Whether the country is a higher rate or lower rate of unemployment in society means , that there are more workers competing for available jobs in the country and less chance to find a jon, which needs a longer

duration of unemployment. For Hong Kong employment market example, nowadays, there are many young people (university students) choose to study monetary subject to do bank jobs, or seek further monetary , share investment monetary related occupations to work. Hence, there are more monetary related subject, e.g. finance, accounting university graduate students compete for any available monetary related jobs in HK, but in fact, HK monetary related investment jobs number is not enough or supply shortage.

It depends on macro economic environment whether there are many overseas investors choose to set up their businesses in HK or there are less overseas investors choose to set up their businesses in HK. So, if the year, there was less overseas investors number in HK. Then , it may cause any kinds of monetary related jobs number as less to supply in HK job market. If the year, there were a many monetary subject graduate students increased. It causes the effect of a longer duration of unemployment to the year monetary subject university graduate students in HK. Then, the any related monetary crime cases may also increase , due to these HK monetary subject university students can not find any monetary related jobs in HK easily. They do not want to find other jobs to replace monetary jobs, it may be due to low salary is paid, unsatisfactory workin environment, without monetary job duties practice chance satisfies their further career development need. If HK macro economic environment was continue poor after the year. It kept to two year, threee years, even more than five years poor macro economic period. Then, the overseas investors number to HK will decrease, even many HK overseas investors also planned to forgive their businesses to be close in HK. It means that they choose to close their HK businesses and their offices were left. Then, it will influence any HK monetary related jobs number will reduce, but as the same time every year, HK monetary major subject unviersity students number is also increasing. Consequently, it will cause or influence any kinds of monetary crime cases will be increased to HK by the long term unemployment to many HK university major monetary subject graduate students factor.

(2) A high rate of separations (people leaving jobs) means that there are more job opening, so the duration of unemployment decreases. It means that when the country has there working people often change old jobs or they planned to find new jobs to replace current jobs or they expect to change another new jobs reasons. It implies that the country's economy is improving or better to compare before. There are more job openings, many

employers create different kinds of new jobs to satisfy their businesses needs. So the duration of unemployment will be influenced to decrease in possible. Because many new creative jobs number is caused. Working people have much chance to attempt to find another new jobs to replace their current jobs in the country.

Even, some working people are doing one job, which can give reasonable wage and it can have more promotion chance in this current job. They will still choose to find another new jobs , it may be that they feel there are many new creative jobs , which can bring new exciting feeling, which can bring nre exciting feeing , more satisfactory feeling , more fun feeling , more successful feeling, more interesting feeling to compare their current jobs . So, it is not only higher salary factor to influence them to change current jobs.

For US job market example, US macro economic environment has been improving very good, many new creative jobs are increasing, e.g. in (AI) job aspect, artificial intelligence scientist , (AI) engineer, big data gathering scientist, non-manual automatic (AI) controlling worker, e.g. artificial intelligence factory machine controlling workers, in medicine job aspect, e.g. drug researcher, DNA cell science researcher, brain doctor, occupational psychological doctor, space science researcher or space scientist etc. creative occupations. There new creative occupations can supply enough jobs to many US high educational level graduate students and they can encourage them to change their current more easily.

In fact, US , these are many different occupations, scientists have jobs, they are doing, but they still expect or plan to change another new similar or different new creative jobs easily. Because the US high education new creative science jobs supply number is more than the US any science graduate students number in US labor market nowadays. So, it explains that why US crime number is decreasing nowadays. Because US has good macro economic environment. US itself country's any new creative job supply number and non creative job supply number must have more than the US graduate student number every year. So, US has good macro economic environment to supply enough jobs number to any US low educational and high educating level young people to job.

Consequently, it causes crime number reduced in US society nowadays. Otherwisem HK has less creative jobs to be supplied to let HK young university graduate students, as well as HK university graduate students number is increasing, but university level jobs number is decreasing at this moment. So, it explains that only HK society increases crime number easily nowadays.

All of above analysis, I assume that the standard measure of long term unemployment id the number of workers who have been unemployed for more than 12 months as well as they feel worry to earn enough income to support their basic essential needs, such as eating need, living need, but it excludes non essential needs, such as entertainment need, travelling need, education need.

So, when these countries young people feel long time unemployment to cause they can not have enough income to support their basic essential needs, then It may influence they choose to do crime behaviors in themselves societies more easily. I shall indicate how any why high turnover and low turnover countries will bring high or low crome behavioral causes in some countries themselves societies.

OECD(2011) concluded the high turnover countries, abourt 10 % of unemployment is long term . So it brings low crime rate . Otherwise, in the low turnover countries, 30 to 60% of the unemployed have beed out of jobs for more than one year, it will bring high crime rate. It explains that it has direct relationship between crime rate number and unemployment rate more than one year number from the average 1999 to 2008 more or less than one year unemployment rate statistics. It indicates that the average 1999 to 2008 period, these low turnover countries have high unemployment rate more than a year , then these low turnover countries crime rate will be influenced to increase also, these low turnvoer or high unemployment countries include: Turkey, France, Netherlands, Greece, Cyech Republic, Hungery, Slovall Republic, Germany, Italy, Portugal, Belgium, Poland, Spain, Switerland, Ireland, Finland, Austia, Japan, United Kingdom. So , these countries' crime rare has been increasing in this period. Otherwise, these high turnover countries or low unemployment rare more than one year, then these high turnover countries crime rate will be influenced to decrease also. There high turnover or low unemployment countries include: Iceland, Norway, United States, Mexico, New Zealand, Canada, Denmark, Australia, Sweden.

In conclusion, it explains that when the country's macro economy environment is improved of better, then it has more high education or low education level jobs to be supplied to let many young people have any kinds of jobs to work easily. Them, it will bring low unemployment effect and low crime rate effect both . Consequently, unemployment has relationship to cause crime rate rises or reduced in possible in any countries' societies.

Reference
OECD , employment and labor market statistics, OECD , 27 April 2011.
source http://www.oecdilibrary.org/statistics.
   Relationship between a recession
and crime

Has it relationship between a recession and crime? To answer this relationship question, I shall explain what is macroeconomics. Then, you will give more clear understanding why and why recession will impact social crime behaviors to bre rasied in possible.

What is Macroeconomics? Macroeconomics is a branch of economics that studies how the aggregate economy behaves. In macroeconomics, economy-wide
phenomena are examined such as inflation, price levels, rate of economic growth, national income, gross domestic product
(GDP), and changes in unemployment.On the other hand, microeconomics looks at the behavior of individual actors in an economy (like people, households, industries, etc).
Macroeconomics is the branch of economics that deals with the structure, performance, behavior,and decision-making of the whole, or aggregate, economy, instead of focusing on individual markets.The two main areas of macroeconomic study are long term economic growth and shorter term business cycles.

There are two sides to the study of economics: macroeconomics and microeconomics. As the term implies,
macroeconomics looks at the overall, big picture scenario of the economy. Put simply, it focuses on the way the economy performs as a whole, and then analyzes how different sectors of the economy relate to one another to understand how the economy functions. This includes looking at variables like unemployment, GDP, and inflation.

   Macroeconomists develop models explaining relationships between these factors. Such macroeconomic models, and the forecasts they produce, are used by government entities to aid in the construction and evaluation of economic policy, by businesses to set strategy in domestic and global markets, and by investors to predict and plan for movements in various asset markets.

Given the enormous scale of government budgets and the impact of economic policy on consumers and businesses, macroeconomics clearly concerns itself with significant issues. Properly applied, economic theories can offer
illuminating insights on how economies function and the long-term consequences of particular policies and decisions. Macroeconomic theory can also help individual businesses and investors make better decisions through a more thorough understanding of what motivates other parties and how to best maximize utility and scarce resources.It is also important to understand the limitations of economic theory. Theories are often created in a vacuum and lack
certain real-world details like taxation, regulation and transaction costs. The real world is also decidedly complicated and their matters of social preference and conscience that do not lend themselves to mathematical analysis.

Even with the limits of economic theory, it is important and worthwhile to follow the major macroeconomic indicators like GDP,
inflation and unemployment. The performance of companies, and by extension their stocks, is significantly influenced by the economic
conditions in which the companies operate and the study of macroeconomic statistics can help an investor make better decisions and spot turning points.

● Specific Areas of Crime rate increasing ,due to poor macro economy environment influences

Macroeconomics is a rather broad field, but two specific areas of research are representative of this discipline. The first area
is the factors that determine long-term economic growth, or increases in the national income. The other involves the causes and
consequences of short-term fluctuations in national income and employment, also known as the business cycle, such as researching whether recession will cause crime rate rising issue.

Economic growth refers to an increase in aggregate production in an economy. Macroeconomists study economic growth with an eye toward understanding the factors that either promote or retard economic growth in order to support economic policies that will
support growth, development, and rising living standards. Growth is commonly modeled as a function of physical capital, human capital, labor force, and technology. So, when economic growth is raising, then unemployment rate will decrease in possible.

● Business Positive or negative Cycles and
the country's macro economic environment is good and bad relationship

A long term macroeconomic growth trends, the levels and rates-of-change of major macroeconomic variables such as
employment and national output go through occasional fluctuations up or down, expansions and recessions, in a phenomenon known as the business cycle.
● Macroeconomics vs. Microeconomics , what can influence crime rate more?

Macroeconomics differs from microeconomics, which focuses on smaller factors that affect choices made by individuals and companies.Factors studied in both microeconomics and macroeconomics typically have an influence on one another. For example, the unemployment
level in the economy as a whole has an effect on the supply of workers from which a company can hire.

A key distinction between micro and macroeconomics is that macroeconomic aggregates can sometimes behave in ways that are very different or even the opposite of the way that analogous microeconomic variables do.Meanwhile, microeconomics looks at economic tendencies, or what can happen when individuals make certain choices. Individuals are typically classified into subgroups, such as buyers, sellers, and business owners. These actors interact with each other according to the laws of supply and demand for resources, using money and interest rates as pricing mechanisms for coordination
● What factors Cause of recessions ?

A recession implies a fall in real GDP. An official definition of a recession is a period of negative economic growth for two consecutive quarters. Recessions are

primarily caused by a fall in aggregate demand (AD).

This demand-side shock could be due to several factors, such as

· A financial crisis. If banks have a shortage of liquidity, they reduce lending – this reduces investment

· A rise in interest rates – increases the cost of borrowing and reduces demand

· Fall in asset prices. – negative wealth effect leads to less spending

· Fall in consumer/business confidence also exacerbated by negative multiplier effect.

· Appreciation in exchange rate – exports less competitive

· Fiscal austerity – when government cuts spending

Recessions can also be caused by

· Supply-side shock, e.g. rise in oil prices cause inflation and lower spending power.

For example, in US, bank failures led to a fall in the money supply and deflationary pressures.Bank failures also caused lost confidence and discourage investment.

· Negative multiplier effect – initial fall in spending caused a knock on effect throughout the economy.

There were no automatic stabilisers. People were made unemployed and so started spending less themselves. For example , causes of UK recessions1981 recession was caused by:

1.High value of the pound which made exports more expensive and reduced demand for exports.This recession particularly impacted on British manufacturing. The Pound soared due to the discovery of North Sea Oil but also the high interest rates.

2.High-interest rates. In 1979, inflation in the UK was over 15%. The new Conservative government was committed to reducing high inflation they inherited. They pursued a tight monetary policy (higher interest rates) and tight fiscal policy (higher taxes, lower government spending. This reduced inflation but at the cost of falling spending, investment and output.interest-rates.

3.Tight Fiscal Policy. To control inflation the government were committed to reducing the levels of Government borrowing.
This was influenced by Monetarist beliefs that controlling excess government borrowing was essential to the economy. Therefore the government increased taxes which reduced the disposable income of consumers and therefore reduced consumer spending.

A recession occurs when there is a fall in economic growth for two consecutive quarters. However, if growth is very low there will be increased spare capacity and increased unemployment; people will feel there is a recession. A key feature in determining the rate of economic growth is the level of consumer and business confidence. If confidence was high then higher interest rates may not reduce demand. However if confidence is low and people fear they may be made unemployed, then they will start spending less, causing AD to fall (or increase at a slower rate). Therefore this shows that expectations are very important and it is possible for "people to talk themselves into a recession".

For an important feature of the UK economy is international trade case. Therefore the UK would be affected by a global recession. For example, a recession in the EU would cause a fall in demand for UK exports reducing our AD (EU accounts for 60% of our trade, therefore, is important). Also, a recession in other countries would affect economic confidence if people see the US in a recession they are worried and will spend less. However, a global recession may not cause a recession in the UK if domestic demand remains high.

Classical economists believe that any fall in Real GDP will be temporary and will end when labour markets adjust to the new price level. Classical economists argue that if there is a fall in AD then, in the short term, there will be a fall in real GDP However in the great depression of 1930s Keynes was very critical of this classical view he said that the long period of negative growth showed that markets do not automatically clear he argued that this was for various reasons.

1.Wages are sticky downwards. Firms should cut wages to reflect lower prices but in reality, workers are very resistant to cuts in nominal wages.

2.If wages were cut in response to unemployment, workers would have less spending power, therefore AD would continue
to fall.

● Can economic crises bring rise in crime ?

Crime may peak during economic crises,
During periods of economic stress, the incidence of robbery may double, and homicide and motor vehicle theft also increase.While a consistent relationship between specific crimes and specific economic factors could not be established, the evidence shows that crime is linked to the economic climate. Such findings are consistent with criminal motivation theory, which suggests that economic stress causes an increase in criminal behaviour. The available data do not, however, support the theory of criminal opportunity, which suggests that decreased levels of production and consumption may reduce some types of crime, such as property crime, by creating fewer potential crime targets."The presence of youth gangs, the availability of weapons and potential targets, drug and alcohol consumption and the effectiveness of law enforcement all play a significant role in enabling or restraining overall crime levels",

● Relationship between a recession and crime

Criminologists say bad economies create more crime; economists say the opposite. But recent data reveals neither explanation is right.
I've been wondering if hard economic times would cause people to commit more crimes.
For example, areas with chronic poverty and unemployment tend to have high rates of child neglect and abuse. Child neglect and abuse greatly increase the risk of juveniles getting involved in crime.So areas with high rates of unemployment cop a double whammy. Their crime rates are higher because of the direct effect of unemployment and its long-term indirect effects as well.

Will the current recession produce an increase in crime? If the recession doesn't last long, there may be no effect at all.
But if the recession is deep and the pool of young long-term unemployed rises, there is every reason to expect an increase in crime.
Moreover, if this happens, the effects may last a long while. The longer you are out of work, the harder it is to find a job, and the more attractive crime becomes as an alternative source of income. And what happens this recession depends on still more factors, the most important being the income that can be earned from crime e.g.selling illegal drugs. Many thoughtful observers think that we put too many offenders in prison for too long. For some criminals, such as low-level drug dealers and former inmates returned to prison for parole violations, that may be so. The difference

results not from willingness to send convicted offenders to prison in many countries' legal system

● May Economic crises trigger rise in crime ?

For the same offense, you will spend more time in prison here than in England. Canada has seen roughly the same decline in crime,
but its imprisonment rate has been relatively flat for at least two decades. Another possible reason for reduced crime is that potential
victims may have become better at protecting themselves by equipping their homes with burglar alarms, installing extra locks on their cars, and moving into safer buildings or even safer neighborhoods.

We have only the faintest idea, however, about how common these trends are or what effects on crime they may have. Are their crime behaviors caused by economic crises ?
How to explain complex link between recession and crime? For In the Environmental Protection Agency example, required oil companies to stop putting lead in gasoline. At the same time, lead in paint was banned for any new home though old buildings still have lead paint, which children can absorb.

● Why do recessions at labour market entry matter for crime? So, why is it that youth who graduate during recessions are more likely to engage in crime?

Those who leave school during a recession, when youth unemployment rates are particularly high, struggle to find a job but do not yet have financial insurance. Knock-on effects can then lead to criminal careers for the young. On the other hand, those who have criminal records early on in their career may reduce their job opportunities and expected returns in the legal labour market see. However , I agree that crime is not only a feature of the teenage years — crime rates decrease with age but do not disappear subsequently. That suggests that there is an initial effect but criminal activity is somewhat persistent over the life cycle.

● Can that persistence be explained by the long-term impact of recessions?

A typical recession leads to a 5 percentage points higher than normal unemployment rate.What is the long-term impact of graduating into such conditions? Our empirical analysis of the link between crime and unemployment at labour market entry is based on a variety of US and UK cohort and individual level data sources. We exploit cohort level data for both countries to estimate the average effect of initial labour market

conditions on criminal activity of cohorts that enter the labour market at different points
in time, taking into account differences in cohort composition.

● Is crime Rates increasing during recessions?

A recession is a significant decline in economic activity spread across the economy, lasting more than a few months, normally visible in production, employment, real income, and other indicators. A recession begins when the economy reaches a peak of. Have they the relationship between economic indicators and crime rates in terms of whether there is a correlation between a given indicator and crime? A positive correlation exists when increases in one variable are accompanied by increases in another variable. A negative correlation, on the other hand, occurs when increases in one variable are accompanied by decreases in another variable.

One important concept is the idea that correlation does not imply causation; the presence of two sets of data (two variables) showing similar trends does not indicate that changes in one variable cause any visible changes in the other. Instead, a correlation shows that changes in one variable can, to some extent, predict changes in another variable. For instance, while some neighborhoods may exhibit a relationship between certain types of crime and the economy, other neighborhoods may exhibit a relationship between different types of crime and the economy or may not exhibit a relationship at all.

Consequently, researchers tend to use individual economic indicators, such as the unemployment rate, as a proxy for the state of the economy. However, any given indicator may not be generalizable to the state of the economy as a whole during any one given recession or across recessions.Despite the limitations in using specific economic variables as proxies for a complex economic state, this methodology does allow researchers to isolate variables and analyze their individual.Generalizability is typically defined as the extent to which the results generated by a variable being studied can be applied to other settings, times, or groups of subjects and be expected to deliver a similar outcome. Specifically, during the most recent economic downturn, many referred to the
unemployment rate and the proportion of home foreclosures as proxies for economic health.

● What are the real factors cause the changes in the crime rates?

Impact of Unemployment on Crime
the unemployment rate is one of the most widely referenced economic

indicators. In discussions of potential impacts of the economy on crime rates, many scholars and policy makers use the unemployment rate as a proxy for economic strength. Congress has shown interest in the relationship between the economy—unemployment, in particular—and crime rates since the 1970s. The most recent recession, which was accompanied by a rise in the unemployment rate, once again focused attention on the relationship between unemployment and crime rates.

Researchers and scholars have several theories concerning the relationship between
unemployment and crime. One of these theories, the economic theory of crime, assumes that people make rational choices between legitimate activities and criminal activities as a source of economic gain. More specifically, the comparison is between the economic benefit of legitimate work versus that of violent or property crime, after accounting for crime-related costs such as incarceration. Although the theory was originally formulated with an application to all crimes, many researchers have used it in discussions of unemployment and property crime. This theory predicts a positive correlation between unemployment and property crime; in other words, that increases in the unemployment rate will be correlated with increases in property crime rates. The reason for this positive correlation, according to the economic model, is that during periods when there are fewer opportunities for legitimate income, people may turn to illegal activities, while when more jobs are available, the risks of committing a crime may be weighed against the opportunity for legitimate work.

Were a direct link between unemployment and the property crime rate, varying one would
necessarily vary the other? The lack of conclusive evidence for a strong, or even significant,correlation between the two suggests that the unemployment rate may have an indirect relationship with the property crime rate. Although unemployment is correlated with overall economic conditions, it may not fully capture other key economic indicators such as work hours, employment stability, and wages. Some researchers, for example, have found that employment stability and wages may correlate more strongly with the property crime rate than does unemployment.

crime influences consumer behavior

What is economic theories of crime ?This brief literature review highlights three key economic frameworks that can be used to explain a persistent social problem n modern society, crime and delinquency: the rational model, the present-oriented or myopic model, and the radical political

economic model. Based on a cost-benefit analysis, an individuals decision to engage in crime in the rational model is consistent n the short-and long-term. Present-oriented individuals, however, focus on the short-term benefits without particular concern

for the long-term consequences of their actions. The radical political economic model focuses on the following key political and socio-economic factors that sustain crime: relative deprivation, poverty and inequality, unemployment, and class conflict.The conclusion includes a conceptual map integrating the three frameworks.

Some economists and crime psychologists believe that crime is not limited to certain areas or to certain socioeconomic classes f society. Criminal activities take many forms, including theft, homicide,assault, fraud, embezzlement, and blackmail. So why does crime persist? Are there underlying factors that can explain criminal behavior? Can we lower

the incentives for criminal behavior? Do criminals take opportunity costs of ommitting a crime into account? The social science field has long been interested in these questions.

This literature review focuses on the discipline of economics and its ssumptions about individual decisions to commit crime. The standard assumption

is that individuals who commit crimes are rational decision makers who expect to gain something from criminal activity, and this gain is greater than the expected costs associated with being caught. Most of the research n this area focuses on the effects of incentives to engage in criminal behavior and on the use of cost-benefit analysis to assess alternative policies to reduce crime. However, not all crime can be categorized as rational behavior. Socioeconomic factors are also assumed to affect crime, and alternative theories to explain criminal activities are used to challenge

the standard assumption of rational behavior.

The main objective of this review is to identify the key economic frameworks that are used to explain crime and delinquency. The three key frameworks include the rational model of crime, the present-oriented or myopic

model of crime, and the radical political economic model of crime.

Economists have begun to question whether the standard assumption of rational behavior holds when consideringwhy individuals engage in criminal activity. Can we really assume that all criminals make rational decisions to commit a crime? Individual preferences, psychic factors, and other motivations for crime may play an equally large role in explaining crime. However

these factors are much harder to incorporate into economic models of crime. Hence, there is limited empirical research in this area. It will be interesting to see how the growing field of behavioral economics can help to explain

crime and delinquency.

The three main economic models of crime are the rationa lmodel, the present oriented

or myopic model, and the radical political economic model. Each model emphasizes different factors that influence individual decisions to commit crime and different ways of combating crime. What is the Rational Model of Crime mean?

Economics can be defined as a discipline that studies how scarce resources

are allocated by the forces of supply and demand to meet different needs in society. In the same way, economists argue that crime is a result of individuals' making choices between using their scarce resources of time and effort in legitimate or in illegitimate activities. A key assumption is that when making these choices, individuals are rational and choose the best option based on the available information and resources. Individuals are perceived to be promoting their self-interest by rationally selecting options that provide them with the greatest benefits that are expected to exceed the costs associated with these options.

The profit from crime is traditionally measured in terms of monetary benefits but can also include physical, psychic, and other benefits. The "punishment" or costs of crime include the risk of detection, apprehension, and conviction and the severity of punishment. Economists do not refute that environmental, psychological, and biological factors may affect criminal activity. Nevertheless, they argue that individuals are free to choose between different courses of options available to them. Therefore, as long as there is a rational element of choice available, individuals who decide to commit a crime will react to changes in the probability of apprehension and the

severity of punishment .This framework leads to a key concept, namely, the "opportunity cost" of crime. Any decision that involves a choice between

two or more options has an opportunity cost. An opportunity cost can be defined as the value of the next best alternative within the context of making a decision. Put differently, an opportunity cost can be viewed as the benefits an individual could have received by taking an alternative decision or action. In essence, the true cost of crime for a potential criminal is the opportunity cost of spending time in prison. The opportunity cost varies among individuals
irrespective of the length of incarceration.
The rational framework distinguishes between static and dynamic models of crime. In a static model, individuals compare the costs and benefits of engaging in crime in a single time period. In a dynamic model, the individual
considers multiple time periods. Decisions made in the past, for example, impact the decision-making process in the present.

● Is Unemployment caused crime by poor macro economy environment factor?

Different models examine the different relationships between unemployment and crime. Some economic models assume that unemployment either lowers the opportunity costs of crime or that it increases
the need to supplement income from sources other than legal employment. However, how do individuals form expectations about their earnings potential in the labor market? If there is a considerable gap between what
the individual believes is attainable (group experience) and what is unattainable
(larger society experience), an individual perceives this gap as relative deprivation. Hence the opportunity costs of crime may be reduced because the returns from regular employment are seen as minimal. In contrast, if the larger society also suffers from unemployment, the shortage of employment opportunities may still be considered equitable. attention that crimes, such as burglary or theft, receive in comparison with white collar crime, although the latter type of crimes represent a larger
proportion of monetary losses than the former type.

Crime accompanies social life from its very beginning – it occurs in every society and in every stage of its development, regardless of its structure, system or historical period. Undoubtedly, crime is a consequence of many social and economic problems which
constantly change, therefore there are so many controversial and

unresolved issued connected with the influence of social and economical factors on crime. This article is an attempt to find an answer to whether the socio-economic factors clearly have a substantial impact on crime.

Regardless of whether we like it or not – crime is a constant component of our life. The crime level is influenced by lots of factors

which nature is heterogeneous. Among them, we may distinguish the socio - economic situation of the offender. Statistics (not only Polish) seem to confirm the assumption that there is a strong connection between social and economic conditions and the level of crime .

● SOCIO - ECONOMIC FACTORS CAUSES

CRIME RATE INCREASES

Crime and changes in the structure of crime are both affected by such elements as: the degree of economic development, socio - political system that functions in a given country, the progress of industrialization and urbanization, transformations in social structure which are age-related to members of the society and finally, migrations. Transformations may be carried out in a revolutionary way or throughout

a longer period of time, they can also occur suddenly as a result of some turbulent changeovers and rapid changes which happen in a given community.

In the case of our country one should consider political changes, accompanied by destabilizing and disintegrative processes, political changes with the transition from a communist to a democratic regime. Further modifications were related to the economic system, changes in ownership structure and the emergence of structural unemployment .New conditions caused a shift in social structure, namely, new social groups were

formed, social hierarchy was changed, and many social groups suffered economic degradation.

● The influence of socio - economic factors on crime

Therefore, one should ask a question whether in fact the economic situation shapes the level of crime rate . While being under constant modifications and transformations,

society will never stay unchanged. Changes in the number, gender, age structure, migration (demographic changes) also have their mutual influence related to the economy,

system of power, education, health protection, religion, and crime. Poor economic situation may translate into crime by an increase in

unemployment. It should be noted
that unemployment, naturally connected with the economy may have a different dimension. We distinguish between the structural, cyclical, long-term, and frictional unemployment. Because of the social and demographic factors, such as gender, age or education level of people affected by the unemployment, there may be various relationships and impact on criminal activity.An analysis of police statistics shows that the highest intensity of crime occurs among unemployed people who are under thirty years of age . If an individual is affected by long-term unemployment, he or she starts to be affected by the consequences of such a situation, namely a sense of exclusion, injustice, and finally the lack of hope of finding a legitimate source of income . The analysis shows that unemployment brings on crime against property rather than violence . However, it should be noted that the increase in unemployment in various ways may affect particular social groups by increasing or decreasing their criminal activity. At this point one should outline four specific relationships between unemployment and crime as below:

· Some offenders combine their legal professional work with criminal activity. Legal business is treated as a camouflage for illegal operation. In this case, the development of unemployment may reduce the "gray zone" business, as the legal work, in this case, gives a sense of security for conducting criminal activity.

· There is a number of crimes, possible to be committed only during conducting activities while being legally employed, for example: "handing over bribes to officials", "employee theft". In those situations the growth of unemployment will inhibit the number of crimes of the above mentioned type, rather than increase them.

· Young people, in particular distinguish between two options: being legally employed, or being involved in a criminal activity. If the lack of work prevails, the willingness to take an income from illegal sources may be decisive. Unemployment, in this perspective may cause an increase in crime.

· There are people for whom unemployment is strictly related to their living style. This group of people treat legal work as an abnormal situation – those people are not part of the labor market. For them, the lack of employment is part of their cultural identity, and criminal activity is, in their environment, a socially accepted source of income. In this case, an increase in unemployment will have no influence on the formation of criminal behavior.

Further analysis of inter-relations of factors related to the discussed problem may incline to believe that in a period of an economic recession, a higher level of crime against property and lower against the person is being observed, whereas, during a period of prosperity (an economic boom) the situation is
other way round: higher level of crime against the person and lower against property is being distinguished. Apart from unemployment other economic factors such as: poverty, the level, dynamics and diversity of earnings and the pace of economic development influence the crime rate. Poverty has long been the factor which has been strongly associated with criminal activity. As it was indicated by Alain Peyrefitte, "crime is the child of poverty".

While trying to explain the influence of socio - economic changes on crime, a number of changes in the economic system should be taken into account, such as the emergence of
economic crises, periods of economic prosperity, the processes of European unification, EU enlargement, globalization, the processes of industrialization and urbanization. If the economic components affect almost all types of social activity, there must be a link between them and the crime. Conditions, economic tension may create some situations, often stressful situations that may facilitate criminal activity . Initially, the analysis of the relationship between social and economic transformation and changes in the crime indicated that there is a causal connection, but now this assumption is not so obvious. One may only unquestionably
talk about correlation between a group of various factors, also non-economical and certain types of crime. A good economic situation, a period of prosperity may both influence either increase or decrease in the number of offenses.

First of all, it may increase the possibility to commit a crime as the easiness and availability of products make them an easy target for a thief or even a person who has a desire to steal an item without really the need to have it. Abundance of goods cause that products may become an object of a crime (e.g become vandalized). Furthermore, if people have too much leisure, they tend to change their lifestyle – and this change is associated with taking part in or participate in events or actions with other people. This causes a greater opportunity for people to be involved in a prohibited actions and crimes against the person. A period of prosperity may, on the other hand decrease the possibility to commit a crime as people stick to generally accepted social standards and the desire to commit an illegal actions e.g. theft, swindle is reduced. They feel more socially secured and safe. The better social and economic status people have, the lower need to be involved in something prohibited by law. In case of a well-paid job, also motivational elements appear as well as the fear of the

consequences of a wrongful act. In literature of this field, there is no evidence that there is a connection between the level of crime and the level of industrialization. However, there is a strong connection between the level of crime and spatial mobility of the population, and the size of migration.

The internationalization of crime causes intensification of organized crime. Possibilities to commit a crime also change – smuggling, tax frauds, economic crime, production of drugs and weapon, money frauds, prostitution, ?money laundering", customs offenses, corruption. The changing structure of crime, its forms and ways of committing it indicate a real change in social structure and transformations of the social life as well as missing norms and values of

societies which in a given historical period may be observed.

In conclusion,the discussed and analyzed socio - economic factors incline to believe that social and economical sphere of human life is interrelated and interdependent. There are certain correlations with the crime level and social behavior as well as with economy and human vulnerability to commit an offense. However, careful The influence of socio - economic factors on crime examination in this respect is still needed. Causal dependencies which occur in societies on every stage of their development are difficult to explain.So how to carry out on the research, analysis of recovery plans and criminal statistics as well as literature allowed to form a conclusion that people should not only focus on individuals in crime prevention programs but on such forms of activity that would be targeted to whole societies. Preventive measures should aim at reducing both economic and social inequalities, e.g balance the level of income or promote social cohesion. Although various crime preventive strategies and programs continue to be developed , they may only reduce crime rate on a small scale, basically they will not have a clear influence on the increase or decrease in a criminal activity in a particular country or in a global dimension as too many social and economic factors should be taken into account.

Is poor macro economic environment a main root to crime causation Is poor macro economic environment cause crime essentially? Economic Theories indicate the roots of crime are diverse and a discipline like economics, predicated on rational behavior, may be at something of a disadvantage in explaining a phenomenon largely viewed as irrational. A recent survey suggests that three general issues are of central concern in the economics of crime literature: the effects of incentives on criminal behavior, how decisions interact in a market-setting, and the use of cost-benefit analysis to assess alternative policies to reduce crime will focus on the role of incentives on criminal behavior.

However, trend in criminal participation rates in most industrialized economies is a difficult task. Many social scientists argue that crime is closely related to work, education and poverty and that truancy, youth unemployment and crime are by products or even measures of social exclusion. "Blue-collar"criminals often have limited education and possess limited labor market skills. These characteristics partly explain the poor employment records and low legitimate earnings of most criminals. These sort of issues originally led economists to examine the relationship between wages and unemployment rates on crime. More recently economists have also considered the benefits and costs of educational programs to reduce crime.

A related question concerns the impact of sanctions. For example, does increased imprisonment lower the crime rate? How does the deterrent effect of formal sanctions arise? Although criminologists have been tackling such issues for many years, it is only recently that economists have entered the arena of controversy. This is not surprising given the high levels of crime and the associated allocation of public and private resources towards crime prevention. The expenditure on the criminal justice system (police, prisons, prosecution/defense and courts) is a significant proportion of government budgets. In addition, firms and households are spending increasingly more on private security. The incentive-based economic model of crime is a model of decision making in risky situations.

Economists analyse the way in which individual attitudes toward risk affect the extent of illegal behavior. In most of the early literature, the economic models of crime are single-period individual choice models.

These models generally see the individual as deciding to allocate time with criminal activity as one possible use of time. A key feature is the notion of utility; judgements are made of the likely gain to be realised (the 'expected utility') from a particular choice of action. Individuals are assumed to be rational decision-makers who engage in either legal or illegal activities according to the expected utility from each activity. An individual's participation in illegal activity is, therefore, explained by the opportunity cost of illegal activity (for example, earnings from legitimate work), factors that influence the

returns to illegal activity (for example, detection and the severity of punishment), and

by tastes and preferences for illegal activity.

Economists see criminal activity as being similar to paid employment in that it

requires time and produces an income. Clearly, the dichotomy between either

criminal activity or legal activity is an oversimplification. For example, individuals

could engage in criminal activities while employed since they have greater

opportunities to commit crime; similarly, some criminals may jointly supplement

work income with crime income in order to satisfy their needs. A secondary problem

with the economist's choice model, which was highlighted in our opening comments,

is that young people are more likely to participate in crime long before they participate in the labor market. This observation raises questions about the appropriateness of the economic model of crime in explaining juvenile crime.

Economic models of criminal behavior have focused on sanction effects (e.g. deterrence issue) and the relationship between work and crime. In the main, these models have not directly addressed the role of education in offending. It could be argued that unemployment is the conduit through which other factors influence the crime rate. For example, poor educational attainment may be highly correlated with the incidence of crime. However, this may also be a key determinant of unemployment. Although educational variables have been included as covariates with crime rates, they have not received a great deal of attention in correlational studies.

To the basic theory ,economic Model of Criminal Behavior: Basic theory is
as mentioned in the overview, the economic model of crime is a standard model of decision making where individuals choose between criminal activity and legal activity on the basis of the expected utility from those acts. It is assumed that participation in criminal activity is the result of an optimizing individual responding to incentives. Among the factors that influence an individual's decision to engage in criminal activities are (i) the expected gains from crime relative to earnings from legal work (ii) the chance (risk) of being caught and convicted, (iii) the extent of punishment and (iv) the opportunities in legal activities. Specifying an equation to capture the incentives in the criminal decision is a natural first step in most analyses
of the crime as work models. The most important of these gives the relative rewards
of legal and illegal activity. For example, the economic model sees the criminal as
committing a crime if the expected gain from criminal activity exceeds the gain from
legal activity, generally work.

Just as in benefit-cost analysis, when comparing alternative strategies, interest
centers on the returns from one decision vis-a-vis returns from another decision. For
example, a preference for crime over work implies the earnings gap between legal
and illegal activities must rise when the probability of being caught and the severity
of punishment increases. Attitudes towards risk are central to economic models of
criminal choice. For example, if the individual is said to dislike risk (i.e., to be risk
averse) then he will respond more to changes in the chances of being apprehended
than to changes in the extent of punishment, other things being equal. Becker
developed a comparative-static model that considered primarily the deterrent effect of

the criminal justice system. As we will see, how individuals respond to deterrent and

incapacitation effects of sanctions has generated considerable theoretical and empirical interest from economists.

Thus, severe sentencing and improvements in legal work opportunities of criminals must be expected jointly to reduce crime. Of course, this assumes that crime and work are determined by the same factors and that higher legitimate earnings increase the

probability of working. In the early literature, economists applied static one period

time allocation models to analyse criminal behavior. In other words, crime and work

are assumed to be substitute activities; if an individual allocates more time to work, he

will commit less crime because he will have less time to do so. The basic economic

model of crime is static or comparative static in economic jargon because it does not

see the potential criminal as considering more than a single time period when making

his decision.

Early studies of criminal behavior by economists can be criticized for beingset in a static framework. Economic models of crime are typically estimated as staticmodels, though there are many reasons to suspect dynamic effects matter, boththeoretically through habit formation, interdependence of preferences, capitalaccumulation, addiction, peer group effects, etc., and empirically through improvements in fit when lagged dependent variables or autocorrelated residuals are included in the model. Labor economists have long been interested in state dependence, the fact that activities chosen in the current period may be strongly affected by the individual's activities in the previous period.

Flinn incorporates human capital formation in a time-allocation model. In hismodel, human capital is accumulated at work, not at school. Consequently, crimetakes time away from work and hence diminishes the amount of human capitalaccumulated. The diminished human capital leads to lower future wages and hence time spent working. Since crime and work are substitutes in his model, the ecline in time allocated to work leads to increased participation in criminal activities.

In nowadays global labor market, the
basic idea underlying the model is that young men have two types of jobs available to hem –skilled and unskilled – where wage profiles are rising in the former (due to ccumulation of human capital, training and experience) and flat in the latter (no
training). If discounted wages are equalized across jobs, the unskilled wage would tart above and end below skilled wage. Also, human capital theory suggests that job tability will be greater in skilled sector than in the unskilled sector. Given these redictions, and assuming that a criminal conviction adversely affects prospects of etting a skilled job, it is likely that conviction is associated with higher pay and higher job instability. So, low skillful workers usually do criminal behaviors more than high skillful workers in our societies nowadays.

Concerning how to examine the impact of legitimate labor market experiences (e.g., unemployment) and sanctions on criminal behavior whether they have relationship question? Broadly speaking, the empirical findings are that (i) poor legitimate labor market opportunities of potential criminals, such as low wages and high rates of unemployment, increases the supply of criminal activities and (ii) sanctions deter crime. Unemployment could be taken to influence the opportunity cost of illegal activity. High rates of unemployment growth could be taken to imply a restriction on the availability of legal activities, and thus serve to ultimately reduce the opportunity cost of engaging in illegal activities. Although theoretically well-defined,
most empirical studies of the unemployment-crime relationship have provided mixed
evidence. Instead of primarily
focusing on crime as a function of unemployment, they use a richer set of controls, like deterrence, employment status, age, education, race and neighbourhood
characteristics.

One problem with most work and crime models is that they assume both activities are mutually exclusive. This may be a problematic assumption when considering disadvantaged youths. The fact that a youth can shift from crime to an unskilled job and back again or can commit crime while holding a legal job means that the supply of youths to crime will be quite elastic with respect to relative rewards from crime vis-a-vis legal work or to the number of criminal opportunities. From the 1970s through the 1990s

the labor market prospects for unskilled workers in most OECD countries
has deteriorated considerably. In particular, the real

earnings of young unskilled men fell, while income inequality rose. This
suggests that

as the earnings gap widens, relative deprivation increases, which in turn
leads to

increases in crime.

A substantial problem that has been ignored in the vast majority of
empirical

studies is nonstationarity of crime rates. A time-series is said to be
nonstationary if (1)

the mean and/or variance does not remain constant over time and (2)
covariance

between observations depends on the time at which they occur. In the US,
the index

crime rate appears strongly nonstationary, for the most part being
integrated of order

one with both deterministic and stochastic trends (a random variable whose
mean

value and variance are time-dependent is said to follow a stochastic trend)
.The empirical results suggest a long-run equilibrium relationship

between crime, prison population, female labor supply and durable
consumption.

The explanatory variables include the number of juveniles or adults in
custody per crime; the number of juveniles or adults in custody per juvenile
or adult; economic variables, including the state unemployment rate and
demographic variables, including race and legal drinking age, and dummy
variables for year and state. Levitt finds that juvenile crime is negatively
related to the severity of penalties, and that juvenile offenders are at least as
responsive to sanctions as adults. Interestingly, he finds that the difference
between the punishments given to youths and adults helps explain sharp
changes in crimes
committed by youths as they reach the age of majority.

Most economic work on crime has focused on the deterrent effect of
the criminal justice system and on the interrelationship between work and
crime. Empirical work provides some, but not unambiguous support for
the deterrence hypothesis. Recent work by economist suggest that the
relationship between work and crime may be far more complicated than

implied by economic models.

The rise in juvenile crime rates has focused increasing attention on youth crime. This has forced economists to expand their thinking to incorporate such things as education, peer group effects and the influence of family and community. Increasingly both theoretical and empirical work on the economics of crime has come to use dynamic models. Theoretical work is developing multi-period models of crime. Empirically economists are using both panel data techniques and modern time series techniques to examine the dynamics of criminal behavior.

● CRIMINOLOGICAL THEORIES ABOUT why people commit crime are used—and misused, if poor global economic environment factor was main factor causes people do criminal behaviors?

Every day by legislative policy makers and community corrections managers when they develop new initiatives, sanctions, and programs; and these theories are also being applied—and misapplied—by line community corrections officers in the workplace as they classify, supervise, counsel, and control offenders placed on their caseloads. The purpose of this article is to provide a brief overview of the major theories of crime causation and then to consider the implications of these criminological theories for current and uture community corrections practice. Four distinct groups of theories will be examined: classical theories, biological theories, psychological theories, and sociological theories of crime causation. While the assumptions of classical criminology have been used to justify a wide range of sentencing and corrections policies and practices over the past several decades, it is also possible to identify the influence of other theories of crime causation on corrections policies and practices during this same period.

As we examine each group of theories, we consider how—and why—the basic functions of probation and parole officers change based on the theory of crime causation under review. When considering the link between theory

and practice, it is important to remember the
following basic truth: Criminologists disagree
about both the causes and solutions to our
crime problem. This does not mean that criminologists have little to offer
to probation and parole officers in terms of practical advice; to other
community corrections programs are to the contrary, we think a discussion
of "cause" is be successful as "people changing" agencies. Critical to the
ongoing debate over the appro- But can we reasonably expect such diversity
priate use of community-based sanctions, and flexibility from community
corrections and the development of effective community agencies, or is it
more likely that one theory— corrections policies, practices, and programs.
or group of theories—will be the dominant.

However, the degree of uncertainty on the influence on community
corrections practice?
cause—or causes—of our crime problem in Based on recent reviews of
United States
academic community suggests that a rections history, we suspect that one
group of
certain degree of skepticism is certainly in theories—supported by a
dominant political
order when "new" crime control strategies are ideology—will continue to
dominate until
introduced. We need to look carefully at the the challenges to its efficacy
move the field—
theory of crime causation on which these new both ideologically and
theoretically—in a new
initiatives are based. It is our view that since direction. We may—or may
not—be at such a
each group of theories we describe is appli- watershed point in the United
States today.

An Overview of Criminological Theories

Classically-based criminologists explain criminal behavior as a conscious
choice by individuals based on an assessment of the costs and benefits of
various forms of criminal activity. Biologically-based criminologists explain
criminal behavior as determined—in part—by the presence of certain
inherited traits that may increase the likelihood of criminal behavior.

Psychologically-based criminologists explain criminal behavior as the
consequence of individual factors, such as negative early childhood

experiences and inadequate socialization, that result in criminal thinking patterns and/or incomplete cognitive development.

Sociologically-based criminologists explain criminal behavior as primarily influenced by a
variety of community-level factors that appear to be related—both directly and indirectly—to
the high level of crime in some of our (often poorest) communities, including blocked legitimate opportunity, the existence of subcultural values that support criminal behavior, a breakdown of community-level informal social controls, and an unjust system of criminal laws and criminal justice.

To a classical criminologist, the answer is
simple: The benefits of law breaking (such as
money, property, revenge, and status) simply
outweigh the potential costs/consequences of
getting caught and convicted. When viewed
from a classical perspective, we are all capable of committing crime in a given situation, but we make a rational decision (to act or desist) based on our analysis of the costs and benefits of the action. If this is true, then it is certainly possible to deter a potential offender by (1) developing a system of "sentencing" in which the punishment outweighs the (benefit of the) crime, and (2) ensuring both punishment
certainty and celerity through efficient police
and court administration. "Classical" theories
of criminal behavior are appealing to criminal
justice policy makers, because they are based
on the premise that the key to solving the
crime problem is to have a strong system of
formal social control. In other words, the classical theorist believes that the system can make a difference, regardless of the myriad of individual and social ills that exist. During the past four decades, a number of federal, state, and local programs have been initiated to improve the deterrent capacity of the criminal justice system, including proactive police strategies to ensure greater certainty of apprehension,priority prosecution/speedy trial strategies to ensure greater celerity (speed) in the court process, and determinate/mandatory sentencing strategies to ensure greater punishment certainty and severity.

To further our deterrent aims, we have significantly increased our institutional capacity during this same period and passed legislation that includes mandatory minimum periods of incarceration for drug-related crimes, while simultaneously developing a series of surveillance-oriented intermediate sanctions (e.g., intensive probation supervision, electronic monitoring/house arrest) for a subgroup of the offenders under community supervision.

It is apparent from these initiatives that classical assumptions about crime causation are still being used as the basis for current crime control strategies. Some have argued that our four-decade-long emphasis on "deterrencebased"crime control policies has resulted in safer communities; in fact, by most standard measures (crime rates, victimization rates) we have less crime and less violence today than at any point since the early 1970s.

With most experts estimating that about a quarter of the crime decline can be linked to tougher sentencing policies, while
three quarters of the decline have been attributed to other factors (such as the economy, education, and immigration). A careful review of the evaluation research indicates that community-based sanctions does not support the notion that increased surveillance and control reduces recidivism (that is, an offender's likelihood of rearrest, reconviction, and/ or re-incarceration). There are two possible explanations for these findings: (1) the underlying assumptions of classical criminologists (i.e., most people are rational, and weigh the costs and benefits of various acts in the same manner) are wrong (e.g., people commit crimes for emotional reasons, because of mental illness, and/or because they believe the criminal act is justified, given circumstances and prevailing community values); or (2) the current sentencing strategies and community corrections programs need to be even tougher
and deterrence-oriented (in other words, the
theory is correct; it just has not been implemented correctly).

While community corrections populations and probation rates also remain high, and continue to use multiple conditions
that emphasize surveillance and control
(through drug testing, electronic monitoring,
curfews, and now social media monitoring).
For example, in the name of deterrence,
legislation has been passed in several states

allowing the lifetime supervision of paroled.
The final group of psychological theories
focuses on the potential link between personality and criminality. Although there is
currently much debate on whether personality
characteristics play a significant role in
determining subsequent criminal behavior,
a number of prominent criminologists have
argued that "the root causes of crime are
not...social issues [high unemployment, bad
schools] but deeply ingrained features of the
human personality and its early experiences.
Low intelligence, an impulsive personality,
and a lack of empathy for other people are
among the leading individual characteristics
of people at risk for becoming offenders".

● THE IMPACT OF CRIMINOLOGICAL THEORY WHETHER POOR ECONOMIC ENVIRONMENT IS THE REAL REASON TO INFLUENCE CRIME RATE RAISES

This question concerns to how to implement and the development of strategies
to assess community "risk" and then relocate
offenders who currently reside in "high-risk"
neighborhoods to lower-risk areas, utilizing
the lure of new job opportunities or housing
incentives. A final group of sociological theories of crime causation can be identified, based on the premise that people become criminals not because of some inherent characteristic, personality defect, or other sociologically-based "pressure" or influence, but because of decisions made by those in positions of power in government, especially those in the criminal justice system. The social strategies implementation to reduce crime rate increases may include as below:

Intervention Strategy
(1) Strategies emphasize education, skill development,and employment opportunity.

(2) Strategies emphasize community-level value change, alternatives to gang

involvement, and offender relocation.

(3) Strategies target improving
community structural conditions, resource
availability, and collective efficacy; strengthening informal community social
control mechanisms; and eliminating poverty pockets.

(4) Strategies focus on the breakdown of informal social control mechanisms—
attachment, commitment, involvement, and belief—and emphasize the importance
of the relationship between the offender and his/her probation/parole officer.

(5) Strategies designed to target
the turning points in the lifecourse
that have been directly related to desistance among adult offenders—marriage, employment, military service,
and offender relocation.

(6) Strategies focus on the use of alternative dispute/ conflict resolution strategies
that result in lower levels of formal criminal justice system involvement in the lives of
community residents; and on the application of community/ restorative justice principles
in traditional criminal justice settings, including community corrections.

All these strategies are supposed that the country's crime rate raises is not due to poor economic environment factor influence mainly. The country's crime rate raising is based on other non economic related factors influence.

Given the potential negative consequences of labeling,we need to ask ourselves: (1) which laws do we really need to enforce? and (2) which offenders can (and should) we divert from the formal court process?

A number of observers have suggested
probation and parole officers do not have an
adequate "professional base" to do the job we
ask them to do. However, it is our view that
it is impossible to assess the qualifications of
community corrections personnel unless we
first clearly define the primary job orientation

of the community corrections officer: Do we
want our line staff to emphasize treatment or
control? As we have indicated throughout this
article, how we answer the "why" (or causation)
question (Why did the offender commit
this crime?) will determine not only our general
orientation toward certain categories of
crime (e.g., drug offenses, violent crime) and
groups of offenders (e.g., sex offenders, gang
members, drunk drivers), but also the types of
functions we will expect community corrections
to perform.

A number of line probation and parole officers only have an undergraduate
degree, while some have even less formal
education. This diversity in educational background would be a cause for concern if we could clearly establish a relationship between education and the job itself. Unfortunately, we do not have a firm grasp on the types of skills necessary to be an effective probation or parole officer in the next decade. While a number of "get tough" intermediate sanctions programs have been developed based on classical assumptions about crime control (e.g., intensive supervision, house arrest, boot camps), these programs still include only a small percentage (approximately 10 percent) of all offenders under community supervision. If these programs continue to expand, it appears that we will need to draw our POs from the pool of undergraduate criminal justice majors, perhaps requiring some prior experience as a police officer or corrections guard. Such "deskilling" is an inevitable consequence of the movement away from treatment and toward the technology of control.

I shall indicate the developing country, India case example to explain why and how poor economic environment can impact crime rate to be raised in possible as below:

The Economist (2018, pp.7-16) indicated that India Women unemployment rate raised that it had relationship between India poor economic environment and India itself country's unemployment women. It explain as below:

India labour force, women have been falling away at an alarming pace. The female employment rate in India, counting both the formal and informal economy, has raised from an already-low 35% in 2005 to just 26% now. IN that time the economy has more than doubled in size and the number of working-age women has grown by a quarter, to 470 million. Yetnearly 10m fewer womwn are in jobs. A rise in female employment rates to the male level would provide India with an extra 235 m workers, more than the EU has of either geneder,

and more than enough to fill all the factories in the rest in Asia. India has high young female unemnployed number, it may due to many girls need to leave schools to find jobs to do because their families are poor.

However, Economist also indicated other problmes in India nowadays, they include that lacking of employment opportunities.

The workforce has shifted from jobs more often done by women , especially farming, where most Indian women work but are being displaced by mechanisation. At the same time, inflexible and unreformed labour markets have hampered the rise of manufacturing and low-level services, the gateway for women in other poor countries. IN neighhouring Bangladesh, whose customs are not so different from India's. a boom in gament manufacturing has increased the number of working women by 50% since 2005. In Vietnam three-quarters of women work. But the mega-factories that boosted female employment there are largely absent in India.

So, it seems that India's manufacturing industry can not develop successfully, it may due to it lacks confidnece to let overseas or domestic investors to develop any kinds of manufacturing businesses in India as well as India lacks high technological skillful workers number is shortage to supply to India's manufacturing industries in

India's labor market. SO, it explains that India's poor economy and low technological manufacturing industry development

and high India female unemployment number, they can bring India's crime rate to be raised in possible.

In fact, India has many male workers who have been encountering unemployment for a long time, instead of India has many young females can not find any jobs to work in India easily. When India has been still encountering the challenge of

lacking of enough manufacturing jobs to supply to them to do, instead of farming jobs, this primary industry jobs, e.g. farmers, fruit pickers , cow feeding etc. farming jobs. It can not solve India unemployment challenge. Because some India high educational young people had graduated in university, but they still feel difficulties to find any suitable jobs to do, it may due to there are less overseas and domestic investors have confidence to set up

their businesses in India. SO, high educational jobs are shortage in India.Then, it causes India's economic environment will be become more worse to compare past. So, it seems that India's worse economic enviroment will influence

unemploment rises and crime rate rises. I believe that they have direct relationship betweem them.

India's worse economic environment also causes many employees have no preferred the stability of permanent employment mind, they only choose contracted employment or short term , temporary employment in India.

They only earn hour paid , or day paid and they feel difficulties to earn monthly paid in India labor market easily.

For India Mc Donald's jobs example, a America fast food company has taken things the furthest, outsourcing 100% of its restaurant

jobs, Servers, cooks and cleaners at India McDonald's are no longer employees of the firm or its franchisees, but bid for positions at the till on an hourly basis thtough TaskRabbit, an online labour platform.So, most functions were

completed in-house by permanent, full time employees. Many people worked for only

one or two employers during their careers. That arrangement had been changed by a unreasonable business logic.

It implies that some overseas big company , such as America Mc Donald restaurant also can not provide reasonable welfare to India workers, then they will feel hopeless to earn reasonable wage treatment when they believe that they can work in any one overseas large organizations. In long term, Indian will feel long term unemployment feeling, although, they still have fill time jobs to do because many full time jobs are contract, short term, temporary. So, they need to often to change new employers, even some Indian people working performance are excellent. If Indian working people are luck, they can change another new employers very easily. Otherwise, if they are unluck, then they need to wait short time, e.g. one month or three months, even, they need to wait longer time, e.g. more than six months or more than one year. So, many Indian working people are feeling sudden unemployment occurrence in possible. When their employment contracts are finished ,even if employers decline their offer contract continue. So, if some Indians working people wait need to spend long time to search any jobs, due to jobs are not enough. They will feel unemployment , then crime rate will be influenced to be raised from long time unemployment factor in possible in India nowadays society.

In conclusion, if some countries feel their crime rate raising reason is not caused by poor economic environment factor, they can attempt to apply above strategies to solve crime rating problems to investigate whether poor economic environment factor is the main factor to influence their crime rate raising in possible.

Reference

The Economist, How India Fails its women, July 7 the 2018. pp. 7-16

The relationship between crime rate and consumer behaviors

I believe that whether the country has better
or worse welfare economic environment or its
welfare is improved to satisfy its citizen's living of
standard, it will bring effect whether its society's
crime rate is more less. I shall explain why and
how the country welfare will influence its crime
rate to be increased or decreased as below
reasons:

What does the new welfare economics mean?
It can be explained that how the county citizens
interpersonal comparison of utility and social
welfare function to their country's welfare policy
to let they feel more satisfactory or less
satisfactory. Their satisfaction can include
leisure and non-leisure consumption satisfaction
daily. So, if the country can give more welfares to
let its citizen to feel more satisfaction on leisure
and consumption aspects. Then, they won't
choose to do any crime activities more easily.

In fact, economists have used no methods of
scientific research in arriving at their conclusions
about whether the country can provide better or
worse economic welfare, which can influence the
society's crime rate is raised or decreased.

However, I shall attempt to explain that why any country's welfare can let its citizen to satisfy more or less, then it can influence the country's crime rate to be increased or decreased.

Every country's economic welfare was said to be a part of total welfare, as well as it can be brought directly or indirectly into relation with money. Why do some countries change their social welfare, then their crime rate can be improved to reduce really? In other words, a less satisfaction to a man with more money than it will to one with less money. Based on this assumption, when the country has good welfare to provide the low income people, then they will feel more satisfaction on their daily living needs. They won't feel worry their basic foods, living needs. Consequently, the society will increase many low income people , they won't feel difficulty to live, then stealing , fighting etc. opposed social crime behaviors or activities will ought to be decreased, due to the low income people feel or believe their country can feel what they have real essential needs at the moment. The low income people can feel safe to live in the country. Then, the country's crime rate ought to be decreased. So, it seems that crime rate increases or decreases, it has relationship between the country's welfare satisfaction to their essential needs, in specially the low income group.

Why does poor welfare influence the low Income people do crime behaviors more easily? It is simple, for example, when two consumers , they enter the supermarket to make choice to buy apples to eat. When the high income consumer performs to take any good taste apples to buy to eat. The another low income consumer or unemployed consumer , he looks the another consumer is taking any good taste apples to

choose which one is the best apple to buy.
During their apply choice process, the low income
Or unemployed apple consumer will feel unhappy
when he knows the another consumer had chosen
the most good taste apples to buy to eat in the
supermarket. However, due to the country can
not provide the better welfare to support the low
income or poor person or unemployed person
has enough money to buy any good taste apples
to eat in the supermarket. Then, the lacking
enough social welfare person , he will do stealing
apples crime behavior in the supermarket more
easily if he brings one plastic bags. So, if the
country has many low income people or poor
people or unemployed people are living in the
country, they feel that their government can not
provide enough welfare to support their essential
living need. Then, they will choose to do crime
behaviors more easily. Consequently, the country's
crime rate will also be raised in possible.

So, I believe that any country's crime rate is more or less, it has
relationship to its low income
people whether they feel their country government can give more or less
welfare to support their basic daily living needs in order to do any crime
behavior more easily. Because one individual's happiness is also , to some
extent, dependent on what others consume. Obviously, the standard of
living or welfare level of his family is not a matter of indifference to a
man. But we do not avoid the difficulty by taking family as a unit. So,
when the country has many families are living, if there are many families'
fathers , they are not employing or they are often working in the low
income level as well as they government can not provide enough welfares
to support their living need. It will bring that they feel living pressure
to support their children to learn and wife's living need, if their wives
are housewives role or without job housewives. So, low income or poor
families will do crime behaviors more easily to compare single people,
because single people do not need to support their wives and children living
cost. So, if the country's families householder group number is more than
single householder group number, then the country ought concentrate on

supporting more welfare to the householder families group living needs to reduce their living pressure, e.g. children education assistance, handicapped assistance, low income short time welfare assistance, wife short time unemployed assistance or wife low income assistance. When , they feel lesser living pressure from their government's welfare assistance. Then, these low income families won't do any family fighting or violence or killing themselves families crime behaviors more easily in society.

So, when the country can improved its welfare to be better, then it can encourage many low income people have ability to consume. It will bring its business and economic environment to be better. So, it has case and effect relationship between welfare and economic environment and crime rate to any countries. The most realistic general assumption , we can make is that, when a man saves he is normally saving up to buy a collection similar in composition to that which he is buying when he saves. Therefore, when comparing his welfare for, says, two different years, we must , in effect, scale up his expenditure in the one year until it is equal to his income of that year, and then ask whether, in the other year, he could have bought the scaled-up collection of the one year.

So, every country's government needs to arrange the reasonable welfare to give the different living needs people in itself country. It can ask this question in order to evaluate every low income or poor people's real welfare need, the question is : Could the poor or low income person have bought last year's collection of goods? So, the country government can gather every poor or low income welfare need applicants' past year consumption or purchase price, kinds of product information, e.g. the low income or poor welfare assistance applicant whether he had enough income to buy any electric products , e.g. desktop, laptop computer(s), television, wash machine, fan, air condition etc. home electric products for his family to use last year. If the welfare assistance applicant had any last year electric products purchase record, then I believe that he still have enough income to support his family living, because these are not his basic living need. It means that he ought have enough money to support his family living need in this year. In simple, his welfare assistance ought be less amount to other welfare assistance applicants, they had not bought any home electric products for their families to use last year. So, it is one good evaluation method to assess whether government ought give how much welfare assistance to every welfare assistance applicant in our societies nowadays. Instead, how many number of children number to the families, old age parents are living with or without living to their sons or daughters together, how many children , they are studying primary, secondary or university etc. families member living dependence factor will also need to be considered to assess every family welfare assistance needs. However, it is reasonable that when the family has many lacking independent ability of members who are living together, then this family ought be provided more welfare assistance need to compare the family has many independent ability of members who are living together, because when family has many independent members are living together, they must have more income source to compare the family has less independent members are living members are living together. It means that the family total income must be enough to support whose living need more easily to compare the less number independent family member case.

Thus, welfare economics and ethics can not then , be separated. They are inseparable because the welfare is a value terminology. The answer is that it could be such a system was held to be anything, for example, welfare or happiness, it would once again be emotive and ethical. The subject is one about which nothing interesting can be said without value judgements, for the reason that every country government needs take a moral interest in welfare and happiness to let it poor people or low income people feel less living pressure, when they can feel their government is really considerate their living needs. Also if we propose to use a certain criterion for an increase the economic welfare of an individual, then the country ought can raise the poor or low income people's consumption ability or consumption desires. Consequently, when their consumption behaviors are encouraged to raise any kinds of products are sold easily from them. The country's economy will be improved to be better. Then, the stealing crime cases will also cause to be decreased directly.

In conclusion, I believe that these above cases can explain that why it have direct relationship between welfare economy and consumer behavior and crime rate. Every country government ought considerate how to arrange the reasonable welfare level to satisfy the different real welfare need applicants' real living needs in order to avoid unfair welfare assistance treatment to let every welfare assistance applicant feel unfair and angry to themselves country government. Thus, welfare economy has real relationship to influence every country's consumer behaviors or consumption desires to be increase or decrease as well as their crime behavioral causation.

economic methods measure traveller behaviors

CHAPTER FIVE

Airport environment influences traveller behaviors

Airport actual functionality

Instead of airport is one arrical and leaving terminal station place main function for any travelling passengers after the airplances had landed on the country airport's subway. I feel that airport has also another main functions. It can help the country to attract more travellers to choose to go to the country to travel as well as it can persuade them to raise consumption desire in their whole journeys after they leave the travelling country's airport if they feel the country airport's service performance can satisfy their short time staying need. I shall explain why any countries' airports can influence travellers' travelling destinations and travelling shopping choices to be increased or decreased.

The future airport will be the assistance role to assist tourim industry development. The factors include, for example, safety and terrorism control, when the travellers feel the country's airport is safe to stay when they catch air planes to arrive the coutry first time. Then, the country's airport can build safe image to let them to feel the country is safe to travel indirectly, traditional cirport service providers will need to seek new service way to deliver value, such as subscription based service models can let travellers to feel the country's airport can provide one comfortable and enjoyable short term travelling staying environment in the country's airport. Then, they bring pleasant emotion to prepare their journey trip after they leave the airport in the foreign country.

So, if the country's airport can let the travellers feel safe and comfortable , then it can bring new exciting and enjoyable feeling to the country's image. Because airport will be any travellers' first time arrival place after they catch airplanes to arrive another country. So, positive or negative airport's image will influence travellers how they feel whether the country , it is worth to choose to travel indirectly. However, airports need have good facilities to satisfy any related airplane service employees or any airport food or product businesses need, instead of travellers' need. For example, it needs have good allocation of terminals and access to facilities , they will be managed and regularly reviewed and regarded their good facility availability , capacity constraints and the best use of available facilities to satisfy any food or product sale shops' sale need and airport passengers' purchase need both in airports or airplane pilots, airplace service employees, irport security employees' comfortable working environment need.

However, airport inside and outside also needs to be arranged enough parking space facilities to let any aircraft parked or stored at the airport from the place where it is parked or stored in order to let any vehicles to be parked in airports or ouside airports easily and conveniently. When any sudden emergency matters occurred, the aircraft subjects to unforeseen operational delays , it should need to contact airport operations control centre to indicate when the expected time of arrival and departure is, there is no need to request a new slot in cases of unforeseen operational delays where the operation will take place within 24 hours of the agreed slot time. For example, of unforeseen operational delays include aircraft technical issues or weather conditions that could not have been planned for. Hence, operationally delayed aircraft must utilise slots in the same manner as originally agreed. If any change to the original slot agreement is required, e.g. a slot must be requested immediately. Moreover, when aircraft subjects to non-operational delays must request new slots immediately, following the correct process in those conditions of use, an example, of a non-operational delay may include delay caused by late running passengers or poor schedule planning. Hence, airport needs have good facilities and communication system to coordinate to any departments to avoid aircraft unforeseen delays to cause airport passengers feel nervous and brings negative and poor emotion to the airport's service performance.

On airport baggage handling function aspect, airport operators must comply with the baggage policy made available to all operators with the airline business management team. For example, where a flight destination or carrier is identified as being at significant or high risk, the operator will pay a charge as notified by management, equating to the cost of any policing cost additional to the services normally provided at the airport for carriers or destinations at lower levels of risk. In fact, airport baggage management needs be checked and delivered in order to help any airplanes' passengers to transport their baggages to follow their airplanes to be delivered to their same destinations when their airplanes are flying with the passengers and whom baggages to arrive the same country's airport at the same time absolutely. So, barrage management operators need submit or demand and in agreed format the already fleets absolutely, such as fleet detail to report these data to include aircraft type and registration, number of seats maximum take off weight kilogrammes of each aircraft owned or operated by the operator, in order to avoid any passengers' luggages wrong delivery occurrence in possible.

Hence, any airports must need to consider above basic passenger service operation in order to avoid any accident occurrences to bring poor airport service attitude feeling. If airport management expected that they have good service performance to satisfy travellers' short term staying needs in themselve countries' airport.

Airport strategies

Any countries' airports expect to increase passenger movements, they must have effective strategies to carry on reviewing any errors and improve performance effectively. For instance, how to keep cost effective measures to lower operating costs and keep good performance on quality, such as for maintenance and cleaning airport cost reducing measures to introduce variable, performance -based elements to encourage productivity gains, how to manage and implement new technological systems to improve information flow and work processes within the country's airport, e.g. airport e-immigration system can allows to receive real-time alerts on any airport building faults. It can reduce airport reliance on manpower in these areas, thus reaulting in better productivity and cost savings for long term airport expenditure. So, high technological strategy system is needed to implement to any country's airport in order to facilitate the handling of more aircraft movements to optimise aircraft handling on runways. Their benefits include reduction of departure flights separation times, reconfiguration of flight routes, and improvements in runway inspection processes.

These new measures can bring effective in improving any country's airport's runway efficiency, developing new infrastructure including the extension of the taxiway, roadway and power supply networks. It aims to satisfy travellers' convenient transportation needs when they arrive any countries' airports and prepare to find suitable transportaton tools to arrive their destinations more easily (airport transportation roadway, taxiway building network strategy).

Hence, any countries' airports need have good strategy to manage a wide range of activities and risks, which are broadly classified into strategic , financial operational, regulatory and investment. Any countries' airports also need to seek how to reduce the occurrence of risks and to minimum potential adverse impact as much as possible, uch as airport risk management strategy. Because when the country has many people are living and they need often to catch airplanes to leave their countries to travel as well as there are many foreign travellers choose to travel the country. Then, the country's airport must need to expand size and raise good facilities, e.g. more automated immigration gantries are needed to be installed, taxi waiting areas are also needed to be explanded with additional taxi bays constructed to accommodate the higher number of arriving passengers , even increasing airplane subways number to satisfy many airplanes need to fly away from the country's airport or coming airplances fly to the country's airport's landing on runway needs often.

So, airplane subways number expanding strategy and cutomated immigration gate fast checking system is needed when the country has many travellers choose to go to the country travel and/or many local people need to leave themselves countries to travel. For instance, departure and arrival immigration control as well as pre-boarding security screening will be controlled for more efficient deployment of manpower and equipment. Moreover, in the line will the trend of self-service options of airports arrived the world, provisions will be made to have more kioslls for self check in,self-bag -tagging and self bad-drops. The increasing use of these options will help airlines and ground handling agents reduce processing times and staffing requirement. For example, a fully automated to reduce reliance on scare manpower baggage check in and check out system, the baggage handling system will also be equipped with ergonomic lifting aids to enable heavy and odd-sized bags to be handled with ease, even by older workers.

Then, the country's airport must need to increase subways number and immigration fast checking service facility to avoid handling passengers crowd queueing problem often occurs every day. When any airports often let passengers feel time pressure to queue to spend long time to wait immigration checks and leave the airport. It will bring their negative emotion feeling to the country's airport. Then, it is possible to influence they choose to go to the country to repeat travel again. Hence, the country's different airport strategies are needed when the country has increasing travellers number trend as soon as possible.

Another strategy concerns airport emergency service on safe aspect. Any countries' airports need have a highly trained specialist wait that is positioned to provid fast action rescue and fire protection for passengers' life safety ,e .g. aircraft rescue and fire fighting vehicles are needed airport. An incident command and control simulator which provides realistic and interactive simulations of emergency scenarios for the purpose of any sudden accident occurrences in any countries' airports.

So, any countries' airports need to develop an internal digital system to ease labour-intensive work processes like fire safety inspection, incident reporting, logistic management and recording of its personal fitness results, with the new safe system , data entry is needed mobile enabled with the use tablet computers. For example, the airport safe unit can continue to enhance its emergency preparedness and rescue capabilities with the successful staging of two drills, simulated aircraft crashes on land and at sea, as well as any exercises validated crisis contingency plans are recommended to earn strong capability in coordinating rescue efforts involving both the airport community and mutual aid agencies in order to carry on rescuing passengers and airport pilots and service attendants whom life safe service when air planes are crashed on land and at sea.

Another strategy is now aviation facilities strategy, it can support fly, cruise and fly-coach initatives, important options to a rising number of interm travellers, if it can be implemented successfully. It can bring enhancement measures benefits, includes the reduction of departure flight separation times, reconfiguring of flight routes and implementation of aircraft speed control for increased runway use efficiency.

Hence, one successful airport operation , the airport management needs to know how to implement the traveller check out or check in service functions when they arrive the airport or leave the airport and to satisfy its passengers' short term terminal station staying or transfering another airplane's flying need as well as it also needs to know how to implement its different strategies to improve its service performance and to let passengers have more confidence to the country's airport service operators' behavior and they also feel safe when they are staying the country's airport. Hence, any travellers' short term staying feeling in the country's airport , whether the country's airport can bring either positive or negative emotion , which will influence they choose to go to the country to travel again in possible. Hence, airport management can not neglect how to improve airport service performance to satisfy any first time or more time airport visitors' short term staying need.

Long time airport staying and passenger
consumption relationship
It is an interesting question: Can the country's airport service performance influence passengers consumption desire? Nowadays, travelling is a kind of popular entertainment whn working people have holidays, retired people have more savings and students need to go to holiday to feel rest time after they had hard to study. They will choose go to other countries to travel. So, " freguent travelling times" which will increase to any travelling consumers. If the traveller often chooses to go to the country to travel, he must need to permit to enter the country from its airport immigration. If his every visiting time to the country's airport, he feels the country's airports' staffs services are poor performance and he feels that they are not polite or rude attitude to treat him when he needs to check out or check in from the country's airport immigraton gates, even he feels difficult to enquire any airport service staffs, either he feels difficult to find them or they need to spend long time to let him to queue to wait enquiry, even he also needs to spend long time to queue to wait check in or check out in airport immigration gates when he arrives the country's airport or he leaves the country's airport.

All of these negative airport staffs' service attitudes and poor service behavioral feeling, they will cause the frequent traveller doubts whether the country is a worthy travelling place and it is possible to led his negative consumption desire in the country's airport. Then, all of these negative emotion will influence the frequent traveller reduces consumption in the country's airport , even wothut any consumption in the country's airport, when he visits the country to travel every time. So , it seems that airport's service performance will influence travellers carry on more or less consumption in the country's airport. Then, it will influence all the country's airport related retail and restaurant businesses' sales to be reduced indirectly in the country's airport.

Instead of airport service performance intangible factor aspect, the airport's clean, airport itself appearance attractive design, large size and shops and restaurants' suitable locations and internal environment design etc. these tangible factors will also influence travellers' consumption desires in the country's airport. For example, in one special day, e.g. Olympic Games day, the Olympic Games country's airport may complete in record time and its airport can successfully handle a estimate record 85,000 minimum departing passengers a day during the Olympic Games period, twice the number on normal days. Travellers and media will describe the Olympic Games country's airport retail shops and restaurants consumption experience as seamless, magical and unforgettale airport staying experience, if the Olympic games country's airport can provide an excellent service performance on the Olympic games period. Then, it will influence the increasing sale amount in the Olympic Games country airport retail stores and restaurants during period. So , when the country is experiencing special day, such as "Olympic Games " is chosen to carry on competition in the country. Then, in this Olympic Games period, it will attract many travellers to choose to go to this country to travel, due to they have interest to watch Olympic Games competition in this country. This country's airport will represent this country's image. If it 's airport service staffs can provide excellent service to let any one of travellers to feel when they are staying in this country's airport short time and this country's airport itself appearance and design can also be changed more attractive and beautiful and the airport's retail stores and restaurants also design more attractive and beautiful. Then, the travellers' consumption desires will be possible to raise , when they visit this country's airport in first time in this Olympic Games travelling period.

● Global air transport network requirement

In the future, if the country has a strong and affordable global air transport network, it will bring more advantages. Due to many travellers expect to catch air planes which can fly to another country in short time , it can reduce accidents occurrence chance on sky or on sea. So, short time flying can be more attract to compare long time flying. So, it explains that why many travellers prefer to choose one way flying more than transfering another /other air plane(s) flying. Although, they need to pay more air ticket fee. So, if the country's airport can have more subways number and large subways areas to let many arrival air planes and leaving air planes need to fly from land or fly to land in the country's airport frequently. Then, the travellers can buy any air tickets to book same day or next day or later day flught time to fly to any country to travel more easily, when the country's airport has large area size and many subways to let many airplanes can stay in its aircraft subways in same time. Then, the country's airport flight frequency will increase , it means that there are many travellers can catch airplances to fly to other countries in any time very easily from themseleves country's airport. It is time-sensitive feeling to let the country's travellers, they can feel to fly to other countries to travel in short day. They do not need delay to fly to any countries, when the flight airline is either full seat or the time can not permit any air places land on the country's subways.

So, none delaying time sensitive travelling frequent flught model will be one attractive flight flying method to influence the country's travellers choose to frequent travelling behavior. Because they do not change their travelling day, due to airplanes have no enough seats supply or the country's airport has no enough land subways to let any airplanes to stay to cause delaying their flight travelling booking seat day expectly.

So, airport is similar to airline to need to use different customer relationship management to attract returning travelling customers . It brings this question: What are the most attractive motivation factors in airport travel market?

I believe that factors may include airport loyalty, various flight time arrangement distribution channel, passenger check in or check out, laggage safe delivery, airpor security service. Moreover, flight schedules are also a main factor influences the travellers' final travelling country choice decision among different travelling countries. However, if the country's airport can build good loyalty image when passengers are staying in the country's airport in short time, it can show a more attractive motivator to increase travellers' consumption desires when they are staying in the country's airport in short time.

Hence, airport 's loyalty seems have relationship to influence travellers' consumption behavior when they are staying in the country's airport. For example, when the different countries' travellers feel enjoyable and happy to stay in the country's airport longer time. Then, their airport long time staying behavior will raise their consumption desire and chance to find any right restaurant to eat food or drink or find any right retail shop to buy right products in airport. Hence , when the country's airport can buil loyal customers relationship. Then, it will bring the advantages or benefits to the airport's any retail shops or restaurants on sale growth aspect, such as : their retention rates will go up easier, their customer referrals will go up easier, the country airport retail shopd and restaurants travelling customers whom spending rates will go up easier, the country airport retail shops and restaurants customers will be loss price sensitive, the costs of retail and restaurant servicing then will go down easier. Hence, if the country's airport customer service performance can maximize travellers' loyalty. It will influence travellers to feel the country airport's retail shops and restaurants have more loyalty to compare other countries airports' retail shops and restaurants loyalty.

So, it implies that any any country airport's loyalty will have relationship to influence its travellers how they feel the country airport's retail shops and restaurants' loyalty. Due to loyalty is intangible and it is obly feeling. So, when the travellers have positive emotion and wheh they are staying in the country's airport long time. Then, they will have positive emotion to spend more time to walk around in the country's airport as well as when they are passing any airport's retail shops or restaurents. Their pleasant emotion may encourage their consumption behaviors to have interest to find any right restaurant to eat food or drink or find any right retail shop to buy any right product in the country's airport in preference easily. Because they had been accepted to spend long time to stay in the country's airport, when they feel interest and surprise to visit the country airport when they arrive. Moreover , the long airport staying time will increase their purchase chance to any the country's airport's retail stores or restaurants in the country 's airport in first time visiting.

How to satisfy customer expectation
for passenger service at airport
When one country's airport can satisfy passengers expectation to accept its service demand, then profitability and passenger number will be influenced to increase. So, airport management needs to focus on how to satisfy any passenger individual need or expectation when he/she needs to stay in whose country's airport for wait to either transferinf another airplance need to carrying on check in or check out in the country's airport immigration gate need in short time.

However, because if the country's airport service can let its passengers feel happy , then they will be super spenders to spend airport staying longer time to consume or entertain in the country's airport. Moreover, it will bring any the country airport's retail shops or restaurante to earn more sale growth indirectly. So, any country airports need to consider how to bring excellent customer services for any passenger individual need in airport. Because its service behavior or performance will have indirect relationship to impact the county airport's any businesses and itself any parking , entertaining services income in airport.

" The concept of managing airport customer expectation on passenger service quality" will be any country airport's main aim. Basically, airport passengers' perception concern how the airport service staffs' service attitudes or performances influence how they feel either negative emotion, such as anger, dissatisfaction, irritation, neutrality or positive emotion, such as happy, satisfaction, pleasure, delight. So, when the airport passenger individual perception is better , then his expected to the country airport individual service staff level will be at the highest level, but if his service expectation is less than his expectation standard, then the airport passenger will dissatisfy with the lowest satisfaction level to be influenced the country airport's other any one service staff by the one airport service staff whose poor performance. Because any one of the country airport's service staff , every one will influence the country airport's image. Of every one has excellent service performance, then, it will let many different counties' passengers feel sympathetic emotion from their every one's behavior. Otherwise, if every one has or most service staffs have poor or not considerate ot not sympathetic service attitude to be let them to feel, then any one of them will let many itself airport's countries' passengers feel the country airport's image is poor. They won't like to spend long time to stay in the country airport, even their short time airport staying behaviors will influence the country airport's any retail shops or restaurants businesses sale growth to be reduced from their short staying time influence.

In general, airport service staffs need to spend some time to answer any passengers' enquiries. So, how they answer their enquiries will influence how their achievement in order to raise the country airport's passengers satisfactions. It may lead a rise in different countries'passengers' loyalty and retention, therefore the country airport can increase many different countries passengers number when the repeating airport visitors , they prefer to choose to go to the country to travel again , due to its airport is attractive reason in possible.

So, any country airport management ought have a policy from how the airport established desirable standard performance, measure it against actual performance to action taken once and revise any unachieved acceptable service level to the acceptable excellent passenger service performance in the country airport. For example, any country airport needs to manage and identify the target passenger segmenation target groups and to make bettwe understand the key elements that have the greatest impact on meeting every different target passenger segmentation group individual expectations and needs from their services in themselves country airport. So, any country airport will have relationship to any one of airline, as well as any one airline will have direct relationship to every passenger when he/she stays in the country airport in short time.

However, instead of restaurants and retail shops; sale relationship will be influenced by the country airport's service performance, airport management also bring more empahsis on non-aeronautical (non related airlined and retail business) revenues, such as shops rents, concessions, car parking service income, consultancy and property developed diversified service incomes. So, airports need to focus directly to enterainment travelling airlines' passengers, meeters, and greeters, business-travelling passengers , users of general aviation services and transfer air plane short time staying visitors, or lone time staying visitors, e.g. the passengers need to live airport hotel for on night or more than one night sleeping before they catch the airplane on the day. So, all these different target passenger segmentations will have different service needs in any country airports.

However, airport passengers' behaviors and expectations of the airport experience depend highly on the types of traveller, they include: demographic characteristics, (i.e. gender, age group, income, sex, occupation) , purpose of trip (i.e. leisure, business), and their circumstances. In general , the passenger can be divided into different group, such as arriving, departing and transfer with different expectation and need, in the way they will be using the airport services and facilities different need and will also influence the behavior of individuals when in the commercial area. For example, passengers who are departing and arriving will require all airport facilities including: car rental, rail, buses access, pre-booking taxi service, check in or check out service, bad processing and security check and vertical and horizontal moving in passenger terminals. Otherwise, transfer passengers will have a short waiting time in airport and their needs will be likely different from those of origin and destination passengers. Some of the transit passengers will need to spend one hour, even more than four hours or half day in the airport. By providing airport facilities that can accommodate their needs, such as a place to lie down and take a short sleep time, free shower, free email public service will mostly give than an enjoyable airport experience. Evem some handicapped people or old people who feel difficult to walk in the airport corridor. Then , the airport will need to arrange the auto -wheel chairs and auto airport vehicle facilities to let service staffs to provide electronic auto wheel chairs to let them to sit down or drive the auto airport vehicle to sit down with them to go to their destination in the airport's any places immediately. For passengers travelling with families may want children play areas, where kids can have a great time when waiting to board the aircraft. They also want the availability of rooms of families travelling with badies equipped with changing facilities, baby crib, microwaved and hot water need. When passengers are on business trip, may want a lounge, with all the business, facilities that they can feel free to use, such as free internet access and other services , such as fax, scan and photocopy machine. Hence, any airport managements need to develop the strategic customer facilities providing service in order to improve the design and delivery of all the facilities and services need by understanding expectation of each passenger segmentation group in their airport staying time.

Finally , in airport unique design aspect, our global airports will need have different unique design to let any travellers to feel that the country's airport can have its unique design to let themm to feel the country airport has itself own airport culture or entertainment features to attract they observe its appearance in order to achieve the increase more travelling visitors number when they feel enjoy to stay in the country airport longer time before they leave the airport. I shall indicate different countries' airports how they will perform themselves different airport cultures and unique design as below:

For China and Hong Kong Chinese airport design example, their airports need have Chinese cultural feeling to let Western travellers to feel their airports' designs and cultures are different to any Western countries' other cultures. So, China anf Hong Kong airports' designs can increase many old big size building photos number in their airports to let foreign visitors can walk on the long glass walkway corridor , when they enter walkway coddidor to walk through different 100 more airplane leaving and arriving gates number and the ground floor is built from heavy glass material. So , any one foreign traveller need to walk through on the long glass walkway corridor to pass any one gates to arrive his/her airplane leaving and arriving gate location and catch airplance to fly. Also, the glass walkway ground floor can let them to see the airport's vehicles and airplanes and people and trees outside environment clearly when they are walking on the airports' all glass material manual made ground floor. It will let foreign travellers feel China and Hong Kong airports building designs are different to the foreign countries' themselves airports' designs as well as Hong Kong and China airports' old building photos will let all leaving passengers feel difficult to forget their old building historical photos and they will know hoe their architectural skills are developed to imprved to build nowadays unqiue desing method from traditional building design method in Hong Kong and China airports. Otherwise, for US, Uk etc. foreign countries their airports designs can increase underground floor fish pool architectural design outside to their airports in order to let any passengers feel that they can see many different kinds of various fishes are swimming. So, their outside large fish pool can let them to feel surprise when they are staying in their any airports, e.g. one beautiful large size fish pool, it can be built to close to their airports and the fish pool can have various kinds of big and small fishes swim in the pool to let passssngers to see, or their airports can appear suddenly and unexpected of a gaping hole in the airport's outside ground, known as a sinkhole. Sometimes, the airport's outside sinkhole will fill up with fresh water to become deep , shaped manual made sinkhole to let passengers to feel they need to enter to the sinkhole and then they can enter the airport. So, the outside large size sinkhole will attract many passengers to stat to observe how the fresh water is entering to the sinkhole interestingly. Then, they will feel surprise when they need to pass though the sinkhole , then they can enter the airport.

In conclusion, attractive airport architectural design will let any passengers can not forget that they had ever visit the country to travel in their travelling experience as well as they can be influenced to like to stay longer time in the country airport by the airport's attractive design and environment influence. The most important influnece, it can influence airport related business income when they like to stay longer time in the airport.

Chapter 8 Emotional labor factor

Airline service industry, front line travelling passengers service workers' emotional challenge concerns cabin crew and airline ground service employee whose service quality or performance how to serve travelling passengers in order to reach service level or satisfy their service performance needs to be accepted. So, how to influence airline service labour individual emotional matter which will be one major factor to let travelling passengers how they feel satisfactory to the airline service.

The question concerns how to let airline service cabin crews and air ground service employees build long term good emotion to serve their airline travelling passengers. Because

bad emotional airline service labors will damage the whole airline employers' loyalty as well as reducing travelling passengers number in possible.

Will a lot stresses at work cause bad emotion to airline ground service employees? The hospitality industry comprises of travel and tourism and the major segments include lodgings and cuisines (hotels, restaurants), transport(airlines, rentals, cruise and railway companies), travel and tour operators. All of these related travelling industries' employees , they are emotional labor, whose service performance or service attitude will influence future potential travelling passengers' airline choices to the airline operating servicer again. Any airline service employees in these service sector industries, have to interact with their travelling clients, be its customers on a regular emotion reflecting basis. So, they must be patient to listen any travelling passengers' enquires in order to help them to solve any problems considerably.

Emotional labor is managing one's feelings to generate a publicly accepted facial and bodily display of emotion. Emotional labor is an expression of emotion for a wage. Jobs involve face to face or voice to voice interactions with clients (travelling passengers), jobs demanding the employee to produce and alter an emotional state in other person, and jobs allowing the employer to implement certain amount of control over the emotional activities of the employees, produce or create emotional labor among the employees.

Thus, long time bad emotional airline front labors number increasing, it will influence the airline whole service member performance to be its airline passengers. However, many airline organizations have their owning set of norms or policies that determine these feeling rules. These are specially seen in customer service industries. IN long term, these strict policies will let airline front service staffs feel stress or pressure, because they won't feel to be punished in possible, e.g. without salary continue increasing, dismissal (lose jobs), changing to another position to do more simple or boring job duties, if they are discovered that their working service performances are not satisfied to their airline employers in any time.

So, strict airline organizational policies will be one strict or pressure emotional regulation to any airline front service staffs. This emotional regulation refers to a person's capability to accept and understand his or her experience of emotions to get involved in healthy strategies in managing emotions which are uncomfortable whenever required, when they need to contact their airline passengers every day. In fact, it has possible that they will accept unreasonable complaint from their airline passengers, even they perform very good or they have help their airline passengers to solve any enquiries when they feel any needs, they stay in airports any time. So, it has close relationship among airline front service staffs' emotions and the airline's policy as well as their service attitude. Thus, good airline policy will build good airline service staffs' emotions and good service attitude or service behaviour to serve their airline passengers every day in possible.

Any airline organizations can not neglect to consider how to build (keep) good airline front labor emotion issue. Because they are any airlines' representatives, if they can build good

images to let the airline the airline passengers to feel. Then, it will influence many airline passengers to choose to buy the airline tickets to replace other airlines because they like its front airline front staffs' services. SO, any airline organizations need to consider front service staffs' health status and definite psychological or mental diseases more than physical diseases, because many airline front service staffs only need to serve their airline passengers and they do not need to move any heavy things in airports in general. They need to spend more time to contract their passengers more than any things. When their passengers give their passports or/and any related travelling documents, e.g. air tickets to them to check in to find whether they can allow to enter airport restrict areas, and if they give their luggage to them, they also need to help them to measure its size and weight heavy to decide whether they need to pay extra fee and their luggage are permitted either to keep to them together to enter the air planes to fly or separate air planes to fly to destination. So, they need to make accurate judgement need to avoid any error occurrence. They do not allow to do any wrong judgement or error in order to be complain by their airline passengers often. Hence, any airline organizations need have good method to help their airline front service staffs to avoid to do any wrong judgements in order to influence any flights delay or customers' complaints , due to their personal wrong judgement to their passengers cause in possible.

Thus, any airline organizations require to enquire themselves these questions: Is there any influence of emotional labor (surface acting and deep acting) on the general mental health or psychological disease of airline employees? Is these any difference in the experience of emotional labor across demographics (age/gender/mental status/work experience of

airline employees influence their service performance? Because above any one factors , such as every airline front service staff individual age, airline service experience, marital status of these factors will influence their emotions to be good or bad to serve their airline passengers every day. Hence , any airline organizations need to investigate every airline front service employee individual background in order to arrange the most suitable policy to train their front line or ground airline service staffs' skill in order to let them to feel less stress or pressure
or they can feel happy to enjoy to serve their airline passengers.

On conclusion, reducing airline front or ground service staffs' psychological stress or mental pressure issue which will be the most effective or the best solution to assist them to raise confidence to serve their airline passengers in airports in long time. I believe that it is the most rapid psychological solution method to assist any one airline front or ground service staff to raise service level in short time.

Airports service environment factor

The environment of airports service environment for the airline services, which will also influence travelling passengers' travelling destinations and travelling frequent times choices. The airport price factor includes income growth, aviation technology and local economic / geographical features of the country's domestic or overseas airports both. IN fact, airports, airports are indeed two sides businesses, it has commercial relationship between both airlines and passengers. So, airports' pricing will influence passengers' travelling demands to the airlines in the country. Any countries' airport(s) need(s) to respond how to help themselves country airlines how to increase passengers number and airlines choices in order to achieve attracting traffic on frequent air planes flying aim. Because the country's travelling passengers number increases , it will influence the country's airport(s) ' income increases indirectly, instead of the countries' any airlines themselves incomes.

Hence, any country's airport(s) will be one good platform to let travelling passengers to stay in the country's airport(s). It means that id the country's airport(s) can build good service image and reasonable products sale price and comfortable shopping environment to attract any countries' passengers feel comfortable and worth to stay in themselves countries' airport(s), when they need to transfer air planes to stay in the country's airport, e.g. one hour to five hours short time, even overnight long time staying. However, if they feel the country's airport(s) are(is) more comfortable and clean to stay, less noise, as well as they have enough chairs to let them to sit or sleep and large area to let them to work in the airport ground floor.

Moreover, the country's airport(s) can have enough restaurants , bookshops, any electronic or other kinds product shop[s, even cinema etc. shopping or entertainment services to satisfy

the passengers whose eating needs, entertainment needs, shopping needs in the airport. Then, I believe that the country's airport(s) can help itself airlines to attract many passengers

to choose to increase travelling times to the country frequently. For example, when the country's airport passengers feel that the airport restaurant food concessionaires will probably provide enjoy positive external gains from having more flights at the airports, additional or better eating facilities are unlikely to provide external benefits to the airlines by stimulating many more passengers with local origins or destinations to use the airport. I believe these airport restaurants can influence the choices of transit passengers whether which country will be their transfer air plane's short journey staying airport destination to fly to their final destinations. Although, transit passengers usually stay to the transfer air plane airport in short time, but they hope that these any one transit staying airport can have any restaurants to provide good taste food to them to eat when they feel hungry, if the transfer air plane country's airport can provide enough restaurants and they can have different food taste choice and reasonable price. Then, the airport's restaurants may attract many short time transit passengers to choose to eat their food, even many passengers will like to choose the country's airline to buy tickets to stay short time to wait to transfer another air plane to fly to their final destination to replace another country's airport to stay short time.

Hence, it seems that any countries' airports' entertainment, eating and shopping service environment will influence any countries transit passengers whether they ought either choose to stay short time this country's airport in prefer or another country's airport to stay short time in prefer in order to decide to buy the country's airline air ticket for transfer airplane to another destination. Hence, any airports service environment will influence any countries passengers how to make transit airport destination short time staying choice.

However, I also suggest that an airport will place a lower revenue -over cost burden on that side of the travelling market that benefits the other the

most. Assuming one passenger
can earn benefit enjoyed by airlines from an extra- passenger using the airport, the airlines will be willing to pay up to this amount to increase passenger enjoyed benefit feeling.

The airport can extract rent from the airlines up to above their allocated costs for providing the airport short time staying platform (transfer air plane short time staying airport) for eating, entertainment, shopping need service of increasing their destination arriving passengers or transfer another air plane passengers number base. This involves transferring the external benefits derived by airlines from additional passengers using the transfer airport to the another destination airport.

On the another view, from a airport location choice perspective, locating or expanding an airport near a city center can reduce or at least contain passenger access costs . But, because land is
like to be more expensive, the airside costs to airlines are serious higher and if the various other external costs of aviation are included. Hence, countryside or the airport is built far away from city center in the country. This location is one reasonable location choice, because it can reduce noise to influence people who are living when air planes are often flying or landing on the airport and the rent cost to the airport's any business renters will be influenced to reduce. Then, their food , product or entertainment service prices charge to the airport consumers will also be reduced. Thus, any airports ought nor neglect their building location choices in any countries because they will influence airport business renters sale prices.

Lean maintenance repair and manual
error factor

Any airlines must need air plans to catch passengers to fly to travel. So, any air plans will need often to fly. Every flight will need long time to fly, e.g. short trip needs to fly less than five hours, even long trip needs to fly more than five hours, even ten hours. If many passengers choose the country to travel, the air plan needs to fly
frequently to catch every flight passengers to go to the travelling destination frequently. So, any airlines air plans often need to check whether they have any engine machines has broken, need to be repaired in possible in order to let passengers feel the airline air plans are safe. If the airline's any air plans have occurred any accidents when they are flying, even the accidents cause any one passengers hurt, even death. Then, these flying accidents will

let passengers feel life risk to choose this airline's any air plans to catch to fly. IN special, long time trip(s) flight(s). So, lean maintenance and engine check is needed to consider for any one airplane to any airline in order to improve efficiencies and minimize costs, maintenance, repair,
and overhaul services in the aviation industry sector, even avoiding any flying accident occurrence or reducing serious flying accidents occurrence chance to bring any one passenger
hurt, even death when they are catching any one of the airline air plans to travel. Thus, any one of airline safety is one important successful factor to any airlines.

Instead of passenger safety aspect, the flying logistics safety factor is also important. The central tenet of the lean to a flying process can mainfest in a variety of ways , as over stalled
and underused inventory and misallocated labour, time transportation and logistics. From a customer's perspective, value-added activities are necessary and customers are willing to pay for activities(Bamber, 2000, Glass, 2016). For example, improvements caused by lean introduction in aviation industry in order to avoid misallocated labour time, increasing number of old broken tools, and obsolute jigs and fixtures. Aviation MRO services have been reported by the MIT Lean Aerospace Initiative (2005) to result in:

(1) Set up time: 17 to 85 percent improvement.
(2) Lead time: 16 to 50 percent improvement.
(3) Labour hours: 10 to 71 percent improvement.
(4) Cost: 11 to 50 percent improvement.
(5) Productivity: 27 to 100 percent improvement.
(6) Cycle time: 20 to 97 percent improvement.
(7) Airline airplane manufacturing factory floor space: 25 to 81 percent improvement.
(8) Travel distance (people and products): 42 to 95 percent improvement.
(9) Airplanes engine inventory or work in progress: 31 to 98 percent improvement.
(10) Scape, rework , deflects or inspection: 20 to 80 percent improvement.

Hence, any airlines' airplanes need to be achieve any one of above improvement at least percent level in order to keep airplane's accident occurrence chance to the least level.
Moreover, airplanes' pilot employees their flying experiences or flight numbers factor is also important to influence airplane safe flying issue.

Because if the pilot has less flying
expereince or he is not proficient pilot, or his flight number is less. This pilot's individual flying factor will also influence the airplan's safety when he is driving the airplane.

So, any airlines need to consider how to train any one of pilot to be one proficient pilot, because id less experienced pilot , he/she is not proficient to drive any one airplane to fly. Then, the flying accident occurrence chance will also raise. It is one critical successful factor to influence passengers' confidence to choose the airline's airplanes to catch, instead of maintenance repair and checking engines factor.

On conclusion, raising travelling passengers' safe confidences factor will be one critical successful factor to influence any airlines' services level, because flying safety issue
must be one important matter to be considered to any passengers when they decide to choose the airline's airplane to catch to fly to any destinations. If one airline can not guarantee any flying accidents won't occur, to cause any passengers hurt or death. Then, any passengers won't have confidence to feel its others services level can satisfy their basic flying enjoyment
needs. Due to passengers' life cost must be no worth calculation more than other service cost. When they choose to catch the airlines' any one airplane to fly to the another destination form the
country's airport. Hence, the influence of human factor in airport maintenance factor will influence any airlines' services feeling level to their passengers because human factor is one of the safety barrier which is used in order to prevent accidents or incidents of aircraft.

Therefore, the question is to which extent the error caused by human factor is included into the share of errors that are made during aircraft maintenance, such as flying
accidents, incidents, injuries, death, damages related to aircraft operation and maintenance. More airlines' detailed analyses have led to the knowledge that it is necessary to study the
interrelation of repair people, machines, airline factory maintenance and manufacturing working environment, and the air planes production processes. Human is the key factor production
process and in the process of operation of technical means since gives new value to the object of any one airplane manufacturing process.

As a factor, the human is not perfect and introduces unintentional error in the system. It is important to develop a system of ever identification and to work constantly on error

prevention. The works and activities on aircraft maintenance can produce hidden and active errors on the aircraft. Hidden errors are a type of errors that are seemingly invisible during aircraft

flying. Active errors are errors that occur immediately and result in immediate aircraft damage or injury , even death to any travelling passengers.

Hence, non human or without human factors will be less number to compare human factors to cause any flying incidents or accidents occurrence easily, e.g. damaging engine, old engine (no renew engine), fire, crash etc. different kinds of causes. However, the main causes of human errors to cause any flying accidents may include: lack of communication between the pilot(s)

and airport airplane landing staffs, complacency (assessment of work according to previous working experience), lacking of flying knowledge to the pilot, distraction, lack of

team work, fatigue, lack of materials and technological support), pressure on the work performer, lack of assertiveness (lack of self-confidence or technical approach to work),stress (working under pressure), lack of awareness etc. different human factors. Any one of above human factors will influence any flying accidents cause.

Moreover, instead of human factor, the flying working environment which refers to the space and place for work as well as the conditions of work factor will also influence human

error occurrence increasing chance, e.g. time pressure, equipment and tools enough number supplies, night shift, all of any one work environment factor will also influence human error

occurrence increasing chance in any flight flying. However, the factors that lead to cause of maintenance error may be caused from wrong information system supplies of equipment , aircraft

manufacturer, wrong working equipment and tools, wrong design of aircraft equipment and parts, incorrect working task arrangement, lacking technical education to the aircraft maintenance

workers, employee's bad personality, poor aircraft factory manufacturing working environment, poor airline company organization structure, working management and control and poor communication etc. different manual or non manual factors.

Hence, all of above any one non manual factors will also raise manual error factor to cause any flying accidents occurrence chances. However, if any airlines hope to satisfy their passengers' flying service level. They must consider non manual and manual both factors for aircraft lean maintenance repair service aspect.

Influence of airside and off airport to airport geographical choice factor

What does airport airside means ? It includes a system of three components: runways, taxiways and agron-gate areas, on which aircraft and aircraft support vehicles operate. It brings this questions: Why can airport airside operation influence passengers feeling to the country's airport and airline services? How does it influence airport ground service staffs' service performance?

In fact, this airside airport physical area choice has direct relationship between aircraft and apron gate areas of the terminal processing of passenger and cargo. They are major factors to influence operations on runway component. It means that airport ground service staffs' service efficiency, used for the passengers and air fright catching any airplanes processing.

Hence, in a geographical sense, landside and airside capacity on how designing and building og geographical area can bring indirect influence to passengers. They need to enter or indirect influence the airport , in special, many flights are staying on the airport runway as well as many passengers need to leave from the airplanes or enter to the airplanes in the same time on the airport boundary. Hence, if the airport has good airside design , then many passengers will feel convenient to leave or enter the airport from the airside areas.

Airports are perhaps truly intermodel terminals in the transportatoin system. They provide an intersafe among air highway, rail and even water way travel. They are an important part of the medium and long distance intercity transportation system in our future transportation tools. Hence, it has enough reasons to support airside geographical airside and off airport factors can influence an airport and its airline flying service providers on its capacity as well as how it's capacity can influence passengers' satisfactory level when they arrive the country's airport. Hence, airport's congestion growth problem that is needed to consider to any airports because when one airport 's congestion is growing.

It will influence passengers service satisfactory level to be fallen down in possible, e.g. capacity is increased by the addition of a new access road, such as additions provide a major increase.

Thus, the stair step growth, it will cause congestion growth because if the airport had used many areas for stair step growth and passengers will have less space to let them to walk on the ground and their airport congestion feeling will also increase when passengers are staying to leave the airport or waiting for check in or check out or waiting to transfer another airplane in the country's airport

The major airside factors to influence travelling passengers whose airport service feeling may include as below:

Availability of enough land for expansion for runways, availability of aids to navigation and air traffic control techniques that could result in reduction of separation between aircraft , noise, aircraft mix, load factor, exclusive use and use of gates , enough airside and outside facilities, availability of airspace, whether aircraft large size is enough capacity and where is location of gates, staffing, equipment freight, environmental protection regulation, and community attitudes toward airside operation.

Thus, whether the airport has enough facilities to satisfy passengers staying in its airport service need, it will have indirect influence further passengers increasing or decreasing

number problem. For example, if the airport terminal functions are spread over a large geographic area, access and facilities have to be expanded to accommodate the spread-out configuration of the terminal or if terminal facilities are grouped together, the access facilities can be congregated into a smaller geographical area.

The capacity of the landside is a function of the terminal design , which has a major influence on the relative to between airside and landside capacity. Also, these off airport factors can also

influence landside capacity, they may include: off airport parking, off airport terminals, urban development pattern, multiple jurisdiction, financial resources etc. issues. The sub factors of the off-airport access functions , they can influence passengers' services feeling to the airport. They may include: user and vehicle characteristics, e.g. occupants per vehicle, separate and preferential guide way subsystems, roadway traffic management, access link to major transportation , transportation

connections. All of these airside and off-airport facilities will
influence passengers' servicing feeling when they arrive any countries'
airports. Hence, any countries' airports ought not neglect any one of these
minor airside facilities of inside airports to outside airports both.

The another geographical choice airport building issue, it is also one
critical factor for how the development of airport cities. It will influence
passengers' service feeling to any country airport. The questions may
include: Why may any country need to develop an airport city? Can it
bring economic benefit and attract many passengers to choose to travel the
country? Can the airport city reform to raise airport service performance
or service level? Airports have become new dynamic centers of economic
activity, incorporating several commercial and
entertainment services inside passenger terminals, when developing a
hotels and accommodations , office complexes, conference and exhibition
centers or leisure facilities choices for
leisure passengers and business passengers both.

Airport-centered development may occur at different spatial scales (
from the micro scale of the passenger terminal to the regional or
metropolitan scale), thus assuming different
shapes and mainfestations. Different concepts to address these
developments can be found in the " airport city", airport corridor, and
aerotopolis (Guller, M. & Guller, M, 2003).

I shall explain how airport city concept can help to raise passenger
service performance feeling in airports and airlines as below:

In general, airport passengers hope airports ought provide these
different kinds service and achievement the lowest satisfactory service
quality or performance level to let
them to feel, such as air transport needs have complex airport
-neighborhood interactions (in what concerns an eventual development
towards the concept of airport city) requires the
identification of thes takeholders involved and an awareness of the
relationships between them. Any airport's main task needs to provide
traveling, air transport, shipping, entertainment services to
the dual market of airlines and travelers. As such, its primary interaction
consists of the supply and demand relationship with the users stakeholder
group (passengers and airlines), which results in broad terms in the
airports aeronautical revenues. Furthermore, non-aeronautical (
commercial) revenues also result from the interactions between airport

and users, namely from agents such as cargo and passengers oriented organizations who pay rents or concession feeling to the airport authority, depending on the commercial arrangements binding these agents.

Thus, one successful airport city, it ought provide good neighborhood transport service to travelling passengers, e.g. bus, taxi, ferry etc. public transportation service. It aims to avail any airport passengers can catch any one of these public transportation tools to arrive airport or leave the airport easily. It also needs to provide hotel, conference service for business visitors as well as retail shops, cinemas for shopping visitors or entertainment visitors when they are staying in the country's airport(s). Also, it ought provide facilities to any cargo -oriented
organizations to deliver any cargo in short time rapidly. So, one airport's any neighborhood facilities have relationship to influence any passengers and airport organizations' service performance feeling between different user agents including: service provision (e.g. between passengers and businesses), business transactions, supply and demand (e.g. between public transport providers and passengers and passengers or visitors) and employer-employee relationships (businesses and workforce , such as airport airline ground service workers). Because if they feel that they can work in one comfortable airport working environment, they will feel happy and enjoyable to serve their passengers more everyday. It means that any airports' facilities will have indirect relationship to influence airport ground service workers' psychology to feel either enjoyable or hate to work in the airport environment often.

On conclusion, airports ought need to consider themselves airside and off airport facilities whether they have enough supplies and innovate their facilities to be better , even perfect in order to satisfy any airport visitors, travelers, user organizations and airport ground service employees to enjoy to work and use their services if they hope their service level or performance is satisfied
to their service needs for long term.

Influencing air connectivity to service quality factor

Can air connectivity growth decreases travel costs for attracting travelling passengers, consumers and businesses and facilities global productive growth? This seems to be particularly an issue when airport capacity is scare or when new airports are added to an existing airport system. What is air connectivity ?

Why does air connectivity raise passengers services? How to measure air connective service?

When direct and indirect connectivity relate to the airport connectivity available to local travelling passengers, any airports ought need to raise extra
airline services to raise service quality , e.g. cheaper air ticket price, in-flight service extra service provision, e.g. comfortable and clean and quiet air port waiting environment
service provision and feeling. However, passengers will generally prefer direct, non-stop connections over indirect air connectivity service.

Air connectivity service can assist airlines to raise competitive effort an offer and they provide access to the many destinations with too little demand for a direct flight, such as minimum connecting time differs in quality , due to in-flight time differences, the inconvenience and risk of missing a connection and transfer time for direct or indirect flights. Hence, any airlines can reduce passengers indirect or direct flight in-flight time to wait airplanes arrive to catch when they arrive any airports. This air inflight waiting time shorten service will attract many passengers to choose the airline to catch airplanes if its inflight waiting time to airport passengers is lesser than other airlines' in-flight waiting time in any airports. It can raise airline service quality, due to the airline has many passengers feel in-flight waiting time is shorten than other airlines often.

In fact, airport connectivity is one good concept method to raise passengers' satisfactory service level. One of the important factors for the connectivity of airports may include: The size
and economic strength of the local catchment area how drives outbound demand, size and economic activities as well as tourism attractiveness are an important cariable factor in explaining
inbound demand (including the propensity to flying demand), landside accessibility drives the size of the catchment area that airlines can serve from a particular airport within a certain landside travel time, apart from the socio-economic variables factor, also cultural , political and the historical ties play a role in explaining demand the origin-destination level factor. All of the research on the factors that explain air level, demand at the origin-destination or airport level is widespread, including gravity modelling (e.g. a bed at al., 2001) and regressions on aggregate
airport demand (Dobruszkes, 2011). All of any one factors may be airport connectivity service to influence passengers' service feeling level in airports

and airlines both service quality.

ON airport visit costs aspect, airlines also need to consider airport visit costs in their route development strategy. Visit costs may also influence passenger choice behavior when
airlines pass on higher/lower charges to the passenger through air fares. Although, airport visit costs generally represent a limited share of an airline's total operational costs, this share can be more significant for short haul flights as well as fair airlines. All of any one these airport charges and passenger fees variable may influence passengers airlines choice. They may include:

Fees variable, landing charge, parking charge for their vehicles or aircraft, passenger luggage charge, security charge, boarding bridge charge, noise charge, emission charge, airport development service increasing charge, check -in charge, terminal charge, cargo charge. So, if any one of these charges influence the airline ticket price rises, it will influence passengers' air ticket purchase choice to the airline in possible.

On airport service levels aspect, for keeping and attracting passengers, airlines and airports need to compete with services that improve the passengers experience. Such service
factors concern for immigration and luggage, but also relate to the terminals, waiting transfer another air plane time, shopping facilities, toilets, atmosphere and space cleaniness, friendliness of staff and availability of delicated lounges. Together they determine the image of an airport and its perceived value by passengers and airlines.

On airline routes development aspect, it can also influence passengers choices to the airline, e.g. Australia airline had developed long route to England destination. Any Australia
passengers can fly to England route directly. They do not need to transfer another air plane to go to England. Although, flying time is above 12 hours long time, but it can bring available to
passengers. They do not need to spend time to wait another air plane to transfer to go England in Australia any airports. THus, airline route development strategy airline planners require detailed, accurate information to make new route decisions, but airlines usually do not have the resources to fully evaluate every new route market. So, they need a sound well articulated business case, can convince airlines to introduce new air services, as well as airport / destinations can influence the airline planning process.

For example, Interviewer indicates that new routes are a huge investment and risk to an airline in airline economic view point, if the airline had not gathered any data to evaluate
whether the new route is worth to develop and predict passengers' new route choice behavior. It assumed 75% lead factor will influence any new route development in success. It indicates these different aircraft type and seats per flight, annual passenger requirements data for these aircrafts: Boeing 747 aircraft needs to satisfy 400 at least seats per flight and annual passenger requirement need 219, 000, aircraft airbus A340 aircraft needs 280 at least seats per flight and annual passenger requirements need 153,300 , Boesing 767 to 300 aircraft needs 220 at least seats per flight and annual passenger requirements need 120, 450 . Boeing 737 to 700 aircraft needs 76,650 and regional Jet aircraft needs 100 at least seats per flight and annual passenger requirements need 54,750.

Hence, any airlines need have route priorities strategy before they decide which new flight route(s) will be developed , in order to achieve airlines add service in order of expected profitability, different airlines have pursued different strategies, destinations can move up the priority board with: solid research and analysis (always) and incentives (sometimes).However, any airline questions for new routes may include as below:

What is the current, actual market for a potential route?
How much can my airline stimulate the flight flying market?
How will the competition react?
How much market share will achieve?
How will be the connectivity contribution?
Will the new route be a financial success?

Hence, any airlines need to reduce uncertainty and risk, before they decide to develop any new route market.

The air service development process may include as below:

Step one: market assessment, required a quantify the time size of the existing air travel market

step two: strategy, deficiency analysis and detailed route analysis

step three: business case analysis, packaging and presenting the information to airlines

step fourth: evaluate and negotiate airline incentives

It is the final steps an appropriate incentive, in certain circumstances, helps airlines commit to new air service to satisfy any new route passengers' more satisfactory flying needs.

Similarly, the strategy steps follow: benchmark air services, identify deficiencies, identify new route opportunities, identify potential air service providers, assess viability of potential air services and prioritize route opportunities and target carriers.

Any airlines may find any information concerns new route business cases to decide their countries flying new routes choice , such as: catchment area profile: demographics, economy, tourist etc. information, airport profile : traffic and facilities information market profile; market sizes , top city pairs, traffic leakage etc. information, suggested service : frequency , schedule, airport routing information, route analysis: market share, load factor, stimulation potential, self-diversion etc. information, any airlines' past flying routes strategic considerations etc. information in order to predict and evaluate whether how many further passenger number is flying that they accept to choose the new flying routes travelling needs.

Hence, how to design to impact either the supply or demand for any new flight routes that is only important because of the country has less number of passengers accept to choose the new flying route to fly. Then, the new flying route does not needed to be design to supply to the country's travelling passengers because their acceptance to this new flying route ends are very less. However, the demand level is low new flying route needs to satisfy these three qualifying services criteria, such as: Are new routes only? Increase on existing routes? Does it work service rent incentives? Will the new flying route be satisfied to air service to the airline passengers and airport waiting passengers, e.g. strategically important? Marginally (unprofitable) self-sustaining in the short term? New flying routes only? Increase an existing routes? Service rent incentives?

How can airports afford aggressive airline incentive / fee discounts and still fund route development marketing in a difficult economy? I recommend that the solution method may include new flying route design and developing and maximizing non-aeronautical revenue streams both, such as retail and duty free, food and beverage, parking , loyalty and premium programs and land development to airport building. Marketing funding strategy may be an ineffective incentive for travelling destinations. However, it may not differentiate a market, as route marketing incentives are used by over 80% of communities in the U.S. marketing incentives can be: Unilateral airport pays 100% or cooperative airlines matches some portion, funding amounts are often tied on the capacity of inbound seats to be available on the new flight (flying) route. By calculating the economic impact of new visitors (spend at the destination), a destination can calculate the return on investment in cooperative new flight (flying) route market.

On conclusion, air connectivity is one important factor to influence any country's travelling passengers to the airline's service quality or service level in order to achieve new flying (flight) route design , reducing inflight transfer another airplane waiting time in airport, or marketing development in success. So, any airlines can not neglect this air connectivity will influence their passengers' service quality.Hence, air connectivity factor is also very important to influence any travelling passengers' service satisfactory level.

How to measure and rise airline
service quality

How are airline performing ? Nowadays, the rise of the low cost airlines' competition is serious, due to airlines hope to rise themselves attractions to influence passengers to choose to use their travelling services. So, different airlines have spend long time to build their unique person-to-person passenger services, which passengers use of different airlines, e.g. digital electronic air tickets purchase method. Any airlines hope to make each journey personalized to the individual will gain market share and improve its service quality to be more unique in order to reach the efforts of airlines to build high levels of customer service appears to have been generally noticed by passengers, when they choose to buy the airline's digital electronic ticket or paper air ticket to use its flying service.

Hence, improvement their digital e-ticket purchase experience and communications factor, for example, if any passengers can enter the airline's air ticket purchase website to buy electronic ticket to pre-book seats in the short time rapidly as well as there are enough seats number to supply to them to pre-book. So, they do not need to worry about without any seats to supply to them to catch the airline's flight to fly to anywhere in any time available conveniently. So, it seems that there is plenty of space for airlines to grow and improve their digital experience and communication method to let any passengers to feel, if the airline hopes to let its passengers to feel that it has unique service to compare others airlines.

The aviation industry plays a major role in the aspect of work and leisure to passengers around the global. So, nowadays passengers' demands to any airlines' service quality had been raised. Hence, any airline service industry messengers are under pressure to prove their services are customers oriented service improvement of performance that guarantees competitive advantages to the global travelling marketplace. So, it also implies that any airlines' services performance will be influenced to cause many passengers feel more poor and let passengers dissatisfy the airline's service performance. The, the airline will possible lose many passengers, due to passengers have many airlines choices, they can find any airlines to replace which any one airline to buy air ticket from internet at home immediately.

However, airlines' comfortable seats arrangement service provision feeling factor is still important in preferable to compare other factors, because passengers must need to sit any seats in any air planes. So, whether the air plane can provide new comfortable seats to let passengers to feel this factor is still the most important factor to influence any passengers to choose to the airline's air plane to catch. For example, service comfortability is how passengers observed the quality of service offered them by the airline's cleanliness, quiet zone, shops, restaurants and business pavilion in functioning like staffs, information desk, and in flight announcement are included as tangible features by the passengers (Geraldine et a.,2013). All of these factors are needed often to measure whether their service performances are satisfactory to themselves passengers service needs.

Moreover, the other factors may include service affordability , it can be regarded as given passenger the opportunity to select from inclusive air ticket prices made available to the different group of passengers by the airlines, as a gesture of goodwill , to establish and reinforce customer loyalty and repeat purchases essential for the airline continuity as well as service reliability. it is the probability that airline will carry out its expected function satisfactory as stated in the flight schedule. Hence, there is a strong link between different airlines' service quality variables, airline image and repeat patronage from the passengers.

Service quality is a measure of how well the service level delivered matches passengers expectations to measure service quality based on input from focus groups. It consists of five factors (tangibles, reliability, responsiveness, assurance and empathy). All of these factors will be identifies that how the airline service quality can be satisfactory to its passengers ' psychological and emotion enjoyable service needs.

Any one of these any five service factors will be important to influence the airline's passengers service feeling level to the airline. It means that the passenger will have more chance to choose the airline's service again (repeating purchase its air ticket). Hence, any airlines can not neglect any one of service feeling to its passengers. It needs often to enquire questionnaires to evaluate whether its these five aspects of service quality , if it discovered any of these five aspects of service level is poor, e.g. 5 scale is the best service performance level, then it can attempt to find its error whether which aspects, it needs to very need to reach the 5 scale , the best service performance level when many passengers feel, e.g. enquiring 100 passengers who give 5 scale to reliability service aspect, before reliability service aspect has less than 50% passengers from 100 passengers who feel the airlines concerns this reliable service level aspect questions to be the best. It is one kind of measurement service quality method to any airlines.

Other service performance evaluation factor is satisfaction in the job to every airline front service or ground service staffs to the airline. Job satisfaction describes how content an employee is with his or her job. It is how the employee responses to a job. It can be considered as a part of life satisfaction to one organization, when the employee is working in the organization. Hence, if one airline front service as ground service staff who can feel more job satisfaction to compare his/her prior airline employer. Then, he/she won't be easy to change his/her present airline employer.

However, some factors can influence job satisfaction are pay and benefit, fair performance appraisal, career and promotional opportunities, proper reward and recognition, work-family life balance, the job itself, proper working conditions, leadership chance, autonomy in work.

Job satisfaction can also involve complex number of variables, circumstances, opinions and behavioral tendencies and a variety of work related outcomes, such as commitment, involvement, motivation, satisfaction, attendance. Hence, any airlines also need to concern how let their employees feel job satisfaction issue in order to avoid their leaving turnover number increases, due to job satisfaction and dissatisfaction depend on the expectations what the job supplies for an employee not the nature of the job.

Finally, instead of concerning employees job satisfaction issue, any airlines also need to concern passengers satisfaction issue because it will have any passengers will choose the airline, if it can bring more service satisfaction to let them to feel , then they will become repeat passengers to the airline.

What kinds of factors passengers were looking for and what were the reasons of choosing a specific airline? When one airline often is complained from its passengers. It will have more mistakes to let them to feel or dissatisfy its service. Hence the airlines needs to find which are its mistakes and improve in order to satisfy its passengers' expectations, e.g. finding what are the mistakes to the airlines' serious concern regarding passenger complaints and complaint satisfaction in order to make the airline more likely to meet its passengers' expectation in case of a problem. Hence, any airlines need to concern how to improve its employees' satisfactory service as well as its passengers' satisfactory service both issues as well as how to measure their service quality whether is enough to achieve general service acceptable performance to its passengers.

Reference

A bed, S. Y. A.O. Ba-Fail and S.M. Jasimuddin (2001), " An economatic analysis of international air travel demand in Saudi Arabia". Journal of air transport managmement, vol. 7, pp.143-148.

Bamber, L., & Dale, B.G. Lean production : a study of application in a traditoinal manufacturing environment. Production planning & control, 11 (3), 291-298, 2000.

Dobruszkes, F.M. Lennert and G. Van Hamme (2011). " An analysis of the determinants of air traffic volume for European metropolitan area". Journal of transport geographyy, vol. 19/4/pp.755-762.

Gealdine, O., & David , U.C. (2013). effects of airline service quality on airline image and passengers' loyalty: Findings from Arill Air Nigeria passengers, Journal of hospitality and management tourism, 4(2), 19-28. doi: http://dx.doi: 10.5897/HMT 2013, 0089.

Glass, R., Seifermann, S., & Metternich, J. The spread of lean production in the assembly, Process and maching industry. Procedia CIRP, 55, 278-283, 2016.

Guller, M. & Guller, M. (2003) From Airport to airport city. Editional Gustavo , Gili, Barcel on a.

Intervistas Consulting Inc.

Massachusetts Institute Of Technology (MIT), Lean Aerospace Initiative, Available: www.lean.mit.edu, 2005.

Economic environment influences traveller behaviors

Prediction travel behavioral consumption from psychology view and computer statistic view.

How to predict travel consumption? It is one question to any travel agents concern to use what methods which can predict how many numbers of travelers where who will choose to go to travel more accurately. I think that who can consider how to predict travel behavioral consumption from psychology view and computer science view both.

On the psychology view, It has evidence to support the relationship between self-identify threat and resistance to change travel behavior to any travelers, controlling for whose past travelling behavior, resistance to change if a psychological phenomenon of long standing interest in many applied branches of psychology. Past travelling behavior has been acknowledged as a predictor of future action. Such as travelling behavior that is experienced as successful is likely to be repeated and may lead to habitual patterns. Some psychologists differentiate habit between two concepts, such as goal oriented and automatic oriented both. Although repeated past travelling behavior is addition goal oriented and automatic oriented. Further non-deliberative nature of habit may make appeals to judge and to predict future individual traveler's behaviour accrately. However, repeated travelling behavior without a necessary constraint of goal orientation and automatic oriented both. So, it seems that psychological factor can influence any individual traveler why and how who choose to decide whose travelling behaviour.

On the computer statistic view, structural equation modeling is an extremely flexible linear-in-parameters multivariate statistical modeling technique. It has been used in modeling travel behavior and values since about 1980 year. It is a software method to handle a large number of variables, as well as unobserved variables specified as linear combinations (weighted averages) of the observed variable.

Whether climate change can influence travelling behaviours.

The flexibility of human travelling behavior is at least the result of one such mechanism, our ability to travel mentally in time and entertain potential future. Understanding of the impacts is holidays, particularly those involving travel. Using focus groups research to explores tourists' awareness of the impacts of travel own climate change, examines the extent to which climate change features in holiday travel decisions and identifies some of the barriers to the adoption of less carbon intensive tourism practices. The findings suggest many tourists don't consider climate change when planning their holidays. The failure of tourists to engage with the climate change to impact of holidays, combined with significant barriers to behavioral change, presents a considerable challenge in the tourism industry.

Tourism is a highly energy intensive industry and has only recently attracted attention as an important contributions to climate change through greenhouse gas emissions. It has been estimated that tourism contributes 5% of global carbon dioxide emissions. There have been a number of potential changes proposed for reducing the impact of air travel on climate change. These include technological changes, market based changes and behavioral changes. However, the role that climate change plays in the holiday and travel decisions of global tourists. How the global tourists of the impacts travel has on climate change to establish the extent to which climate change, considerations features in holiday travel decision making processes and to investigate the major barriers to global tourists adopting less carbon intensive travel practices. Whether tourists will aware the impacts that their holidays and travel have on climate changes.

When, it comes to understand indvidual traveler's behavioral change, wide range of conceptual theories have been developed, utilizing various social, psychological, subjective and objective variables in order to model travel consumption behavior. These theories of travel behavioral change operate at a number of different levels, including the individual level, the interpersonal level and community level. Whether pro-environmental behavior can be used to predict travel consumption behavior in a climate change. However, the question of what determines pro-environmental behavior in such a complex one that it can not be visualized through one single framework or diagram.

Despite the potentially high risk scenario for the tourism industry and the global environment, the tourism and climate change ought have close relationship. Whether what are the important factors and variables which can limit tourism? e.g. money, time, family problem, extreme hot or cold weather change, air ticket price, journey attraction etc. variable factors. Mention of holidays and travel were deliberately avoided in the recruitment process, so as not to create a connection factor to influence traveler's individual mind. However, the dismissal of alternative transportation modes can be conceived as either a structural barrier, in the sense that flying is perhaps the only realistic option to reach long-haul holiday destination, or a perceived behavioral control barriers in that an individual perceives flying as the only option open to whom. The transportation tool factor will be depend to extent on the distance to the destination. This can also be interpreted in a social perspective as an intention with the resources available where much international tourism is structured around flying. To increase the availability of different transportation modes, tourists could choose holiday destination closer to home.

Finally, also how to predict future travel behavioural consumption. I feel that travel agents need to predict whether any country's random daily variation of weather factor is also important to influence travel behaviour. e.g. in weather, temperature, rainfall adn snowfall with traffic accidents factors will have relationship to cause travel demand. Some scientists estimate suggest that when warmed temperatures and reduced snowfall are associated with a moderate decline in non-fatal accidents, they are also associated with a significant increase in fatal accidents. Thus increase in fatalities and temperature. Half of the estimated effect of temperature on fatalities is due to changes in the exposure to pedestrians, bicyclists and motorcyclists as temperature increase. So, if any countries have rainfall, snowfall and low temperature to cause traffic accidents, whether this accident occurrence will influence the travelers who liking climb snow hills, riding bicycle, running sports who will avoid to travel to these countries' bad weather after occurs. So, why I feel that this natural climate factor will also be one serious factor to influence travel behavioral consumption.

Future travel consumption behavior

Whether individual habitual behaviour can influence travelling behaviour : e.g. renting travel transportation tools

Whether habit can be intended to predict of future travel behavior to people are creatures of habits. Many of human's everyday goal-directed behaviors are performed in a habitual fashion, the transportation made and route one takes to work, one's choice of breakfast. Habits are formed when using the some behavior frequently and a similar consistency in a similar context for the some purpose whether the individual past travel consumption model will be caused a habit to whom. e.g. choosing whom travel agent to buy air ticket or traveling package; choosing the same or similar countries' destinations to go to travel ; choosing the business class or normal (general) class of quality airlines to catch planes. Does habitual rent traveling car tools use not lead to more resistance to change of travel mode? It has been argued that past behavior is the best predictor of future behavior to travel consumption. If individual traveler's past consumption behavior was always reasoned, then frequency of prior travel consumption behavior should only have an indirect link to the individual traveler's behavior. It seems that renting travel car tools to use is a habit example. So, a strong rent traveling car tools useful habit makes traveling mode choice. People with a strong renting of traveling car tools of habit should have low motivation to attend to gather any information about public transportation in their choice of travelling country for individual or family or friends members during their traveling journeys.

Even when persuasive communication changes the traveler whose attitudes and intention, in the case of individual traveler or family travelers with a strong renting travel car tools habit. It is difficult to change whose travel behaviors to choose to catch public transportation in whose any trips in any countries. However, understanding of travel behavior and the reasons for choosing one mode of transportation over another. The arguments for rent traveling car tools to use, including convenience, speed, comfort and individual freedom and well known. Increasingly, psychological factors include such as, perceptions, identity, social norms and habit are being used to understand travel mode choice. Whether how many travel consumers will choose to rent traveling car tools during their trips in any countries. It is difficult to estimate the numbers. As the average level of renting travel car tools of dependence or attitudes to certain travel package policies from travel agents. Instead different people must be treated in different ways because who are motivated in different ways and who are motivated by different travel package policies ways from travel agents.

In conclusion, the factors influence whose traveler's individual behavior either who chooses to rent traveling car tools or who chooses to catch public transportation when who individual goes to travel in alone trip or family trip. It include influence mode choice factors, such as social psychology factor and marketing on segmentation factor both to influence whose transportation choice of behavior in whose trip.

How to determine future travel behavior from past travel experience and perceptions of risk and safety for the benefits to travel consumers?

How to determine future travel behavior from past travel experience and perceptions of risk and safety for the benefits to travel consumers? Why does individual traveler avoid certain destination(s) is(are) as relevant to tourist decision making as why who chooses to travel to others. Perceptions of risk and safety and travel experience are likely to influence travel decisions. If travel agents had efforts to predict future travel behavior to guess whether travelers will feel where is(are) risk and unsafe to cause who does not choose to go to the country to travel. Then, the travel agents will avoid to choose to spend much time to design the different traveling package to attract their potential travel consumers to choose to travel. The reason is because in the case of individual traveler's tourism experience, the traveler whose past disappointment travel experience (psychological risk) will be a serious threat to the traveler's health or life (health, physical or terrorism risk). The past safety or unhealthy risk to the country(countries) will influence the traveler decides to choose not to go to the countries(country) to travel again in the future.

What is push and pull factors to influence any traveler who chooses where is whose preferable travelling destination

How to predict individual traveler's behavioral intention of choosing a travel destination. Understanding why people travel and what factors influence their behavioral intention of choosing a travel destination is beneficial to tourism planning and marketing. In general, an individual's choice of a travel destination into two forces. The first force is the push factor that pushes an individual away from home and attempt to develop a general desire to go somewhere, without specifying where that may be. The other force is the pull factor that pull an individual toward in destination, due to a region-specific or perceived attractiveness of a destination. The respective push and pull factors illustrate that people travel because who are pushed by whose internal motives and pulled by external forced of a destination. However, the decision making process leading to the choice of a travel destination is a very complex process. For example, a Taiwanese traveler who might either choose new travel destination of Hong Kong or another old travel Asia destinations again or who also might choose any one of Western country, as a new travel destination. The travel agents can predict where who will have intention to choose to travel from whose past behavior and attitude, subjective and perceived behavioral control model.

The factors influence where is the traveler choice, include personal safety, scenic beauty, cultural interest, climate changing, transportation tools, friendliness of local people, price of trip, trip package service in hotels and restaurants, quality and variety of food and shopping facilities and services etc. needs. So, whose factors will influence where is the individual travel's choice. It seems every traveler whose choice of travel process, will include past behavior. e.g. travelling experience, travelling habit, then to choose the best seasoned travelling action to satisfy whose travel needs. This process is the individual traveler's psychological choice process, who must need time to gather information to compare concerning of different travel packages, destination scene, climate change, transportation tools available to the destination, air ticket price etc. these factors, then to judge where is the best right destination to travel in the right time.

Why expectation, motivation and attitude factor can influence travelling behaviour.

Social psychology is concerned with gaining insight into the psychological of socially relevant behaviors and the processes. For instance, on a global level bad influence to global warming, it influences some countries extreme cold or hot bad climate changing occurrence, then it ought influence some travelers' behavioral decision to change their mind to choose some countries to go to travel at the moment which do not occur extreme hot or cold climate (temperature). e.g. above than 40 degree in summer or below than 0 degree in winter. Due to the extreme climate changing environment in the countries, it will cause them to feel uncomfortable to play during their trips. So, the global warming causes to climate changing factor will influence the numbers of travel consumption to be reduced possibly. This is global climate changing environment factor influences to bad or uncomfortable social psychological feeling to global travelers' mind of traveling decision. What is individual traveler expectation, motivation and attitude? Tourism sector includes inbound (domestic) tourism and outbound (overseas) tourism both incomes to any countries. According to recent article, a tourist behavior model has been developed, called the expectation, motivation and attitude (EMA) model (Hsu et al., 2010).

This model focuses on the pre-visit stage of tourists by modeling the behavioral process by incorporating expectation, motivation and attitude. Travel motivation is considered as an essential component of the behavioral process, which has been increasing attention from the travel; industry. The economic approach defines "tourism" is an identifiable nationally important industry. It includes the component activities of transportation, accommodation, recreation, food and related service. So, tourism behavioral consumption is concerned the individual tourist's usual habituate of the industry which responds to whose needs, and of the impacts that both the tourist and the tourism industry have on the socio-cultural, economic and physical environment.

However, travel motivation means how to understand and predict factors that influence travel decision making. According to Backman and others (1995, p.15), motivation is conceptually viewed as " a state of need, a condition that services as a driving force to display different kind of behavior toward certain types of activities, developing preferences, arriving at some expected satisfactory outcome." So, motivation and expectancy which has close relationship to any tourist before who decided to do any tourism of behavior. Some economists confirmed motivation and expectancy which has relations, such as expectation of visiting an outbound destination has a direct effect on motivation to visit the destination; motivation has a direct effect on attitude toward visiting the destination; expectation of visiting the outbound destination has a direct affect on attitude toward visiting the destination and motivation has a mediating effect on the relationship in between expectation and attitude.

What methods can predict future travel behavioural consumption

How to use qualitative of travel behavioural method to predict future travel consumption.

I also suggest to use qualitative of travel behavioural method to predict future travel consumption. Methods such as focus groups interviews and participant observer techniques can be used with quantitative approaches on their own to fill the gaps left by quantitative techniques. These insights have contributed to the development of increasingly sophisticated models to forecast travel behavior and predict changes in behavior in response to change in the transportation system. First, survey methods restrict not only the question frame but the answer frame as well, anticipating the important issues and questions and the responses. However, these surveys methods are not well suited to exploratory areas of research where issues remain unidentified and the researched seek to answer the question "why?". Second, data collection methods using traditional travel diaries or telephone recruitment can under represent certain segments of the population, particularly the older persons with little education, minorities and the poor. Before the survey, focus group for example can be used to identify what socio-demographic variables to include in the survey, how best to structure the diary, even what incentives will be most effective in increasing the response rate. After the survey, focus, focus groups can be used to build explanations for the survey results to identify the "why" of the results as well as the implications. One Asia Pacific survey research result was made by tourism market investigation before. It indicated the travel in Asia Pacific market in the past, had often been undertaken in large groups through leisure package sold in bulk, or in large organized business groups, future travelers will be in smaller groups or alone, and for a much wider range of reasons. Significant new traveler segments, such as female business traveler. The small business traveler and the senior traveler, all of which have different aspirations and requirements from the travel experience.

Moreover, Asia tourism market will start to exist behaviors in the adoption of newer technologies, a giving the traveler new ways to manage the travel experience, creating new behaviors. This with provide new opportunities for travel providers. The use of mobile devices, smartphones, tablets etc. and social media are the obvious findings to become an integral part of the travel experience. Thus, quality method can attempt to predict Asia Pacific tourism market development in the future.

However, improving the predictive power of travel behavior models and to increase understanding travel behavior which lies in the use of panel data(repeated measures from the same individuals). Whereas, cross-sectional data only reveal inter-individual differences at one moment in time, panel data can reveal intra-individual changes over time. In effect, panel data are generally better suited to understand and predict (changes in) travel behavior. However, a substantial proportion was also observed to transition between very different activity/travel patterns over time, indicating that from one year to the next, many people renegotiated their activity/travel patterns.

How to apply advanced traveler information systems (ATIS) to predict future travelling behaviour.

Nowadays, information can impact on traveler behavior and network performance. For example, when steadily growing levels of vehicle ownership and vehicle miles traveled information has been identified as a potential strategy towards man aging travel demand, optimizing transportation networks and better utilizing available capacity. Toward, this goal to predict further tourist behavioral consumption. Many countries, government tourism development institutes has applied advanced traveler information systems (ATIS) which travel behavior models and high-fidelity network performance models made increasingly feasible through the rapid advances in computer power. Crucial components of this problem domain are the modeling of individual tourist drivers' response to travel information and the development accurate guidance of relevance to real would trip makers. So, this advanced traveler information systems (ATIS) can assist the tourist who like to rent travelling car tools to travel in any countries own free traveler information systems service conveniently. Also, this travel information system can be intended to assist travelers to make better travel choices. e.g. this system can improve the decision making of individual traveler rather than improvements of network performance overall. So, we need to understand how tourists make their travel plans. Also, understanding decision process that lead to booking of the trip is equally important, as it allows of a potential behavior.

How does online tourism sale channel can influence traveling consumption of behaviour.

Nowadays, internet is popular, it seems that booking air ticket behavior of using internet is predicted to influence overall tourism air tickets payment method. Tourism industry has grown in the previous several decades. Despite its global impact, questions related to better understanding of tourists and whose habits. Using online travel air ticket booking benefits include booking electronic air tickets can be made from entering any electronic travel agents websites in the short time and electronic travel ticket payers do not need leave home, who can pay visa card to pre booking any electronic travel ticket from online channel conveniently.

How to analyze activity based travel demand ? Nowadays, human are concerning the traffic congestion and air quality deterioration, the supply oriented focus of transportation planning has expanded to include how to manage travel demand within the available transportation supply. Consequently, there has been an increasing interest in travel demand management strategies, such as congestion pricing that attempts to change aggregate travel demand. The prediction aggregate level, long term travel demand to understanding disaggregate level (i.e. individual levels) behavioral responses to short term demand policies, such as ride sharing incentives, congestion pricing and employer based demand management schemes, alternate work schedules, telecommuting limitation of travel agent traditionally work nature shall influence oriented trip based travel modelling passenger travel demand indirectly.

Finally, online travel purchase will be popular to influence the number of travel behavioural consumption nowadays. Any travel package products can be sold from websites to attract travellers to choose to prebook air ticket for any trips conveniently. In the past ten years, the internet has become the predominant carrier of all types of information and transactions. Regarding travel decisions, internet has also become an important sales channels for the travel industry, because it is associated with comparably lower distribution and sales costs, but also because ir adapts to hign supply and demand dynamics in this industry. Consequently, the travel and tourism industry tries to increase the internet sale specific share of sales volumes. So, internet sale channel has changed travel consumption behavioural pattern and characteristics and travel experience. For example, Switzerland has one of the highest population-to-computer ratio in Europe. It is also one of the most highly internet penetrated countries in terms of use of the WWW on a day-to-day basis, with more than 75 percent of the population older than 14 years using the WWW daily (ICT, 2005).

The reason of booking online tourism may include: convenience, fast transaction, finding traveling package choice easily, more airline seats available. So, online booking tourism will influence the traditional tourism agents visiting of sales and air tickets and travelling package numbers to be decreased. Finally, the online booking tourism market shares will be expanded to more than traditional tourism agents visits sale market in the future one day. So, the travel agents who still use the traditional tourism visiting sale channel which ought raise whose features to compare to differ to online tourism sale channel if these traditional touriam agents want to keep competitive ability in tourism industry for long term.

Actively based patterns of urban population of travel behavioural prediction method.

Actively based patterns of urban population. It is a method of motivational framework means in which societal constraints and inherent individual motivations interact to shape activity participation patterns. It can be used to predict one city or urban the numbers of travel demand in the year. It has two elements: First, capability constraints refer to constraints are imposed by biological needs, such as eating and sleeping and/or resources, such as income, availability of cars etc. to undertake the urban or city's family activities in the year. Second, coupling constraints define where, when and the duration of planning activities that are to be pursued with other individuals. So, this method needs to gather information (data) to get the relationship between activities, travel and spending work time and space time to evaluate whether there are how many families who have real needs to spend time to go to travel in the year.

What is trip based versus activity based approaches?

What is trip based versus activity based approaches? The fundamental difference between the trip-based and activity based approaches is that the former approach directly focuses on trips without explicit recognition of the motivation or reason for the trips and travel. The activity based approach , on the other hand, views travel as a demand derived from the need to pursue travel activities. So, it is better understand the individual or family behavior basis for individual or family travelling decision regarding participation in travelling activities in certain places or cities or countries at given times and hence the resulting travel needs. This behavioral basis includes all the factors that influence the why, how, when and where of performed activities and resulting individuals and household, the cultural/ social norms of the community and the travel surrounding environment.

Another difference between the two approaches is in the way travel is represented. The trip based approach represents travel as a collection of trips. Each trip is considered as independent of other trips, without considering the inter-relationship in the choice attributes , such as time, destination and mode of different trips. As tours are chains of trips beginning and ending at a same location , say home or work. The tour based representation helps maintain the consistency across and capture the interdependency and consistency of the modeled choice attributed among the trips of the same tour.

In addition to the tour based representation of travel, the activity based approach focuses on sequences or patterns of activity participation and travel behavior, using the whole day or longer periods of time is the unit of analysis. Such as approach can address travel demand management issues through an examination of how people modify their activity participation, for example, will individuals substitute more out-of-home activities for in home activities in the evening of who arrived early form work due-to a work schedule change?

The major difference between trip based and the activity based approaches is in the way, the time dimension of activities and travel is considered. In the trip based approach, time is reduced to being simply a cost making a trip and a day's viewed as a combination, defined peak and off peak time periods. On the other hand, activity based approach views individuals' activity travel patterns are a result of their time use decisions with a continuous time domain. As individuals have 24 hours in a day or multiples of 24 hours for longer periods of time and decide how to use that travel among or allocate that time to activities and travel and with who, subject to their socio-demographic, transportation system and other and scheduling of trips. So, determining the impact of travel demand management policies on time use behavior is an important step to assessing the impact of such policies on individual travel behavior. The final major difference between this two approaches relates to the level of aggregation. In the trip based approach, most aspect of travel, e.g. number of trips etc. are analyzed at an aggregate level.

Consequently, trip based methods accommodate the effect of socio-demographic attributes of households and individuals in a very limited fashion, which limits the activity of the method to evaluate travel impacts of long term socio-demographic characteristics of the individuals who actually make the activity travel choices and the travel service characteristics of the surrounding environment. So, the activity based models are better equipped to forecast the longer term changes in travel demand in response composition and the travel environment of urban areas. Also, using activity based models, the impact of policies can be assessed by predicting individual level behavioral responses instead of employing trip based statistical averages that are aggregated over defined demographic segments.

Why senior age will be main travelling target.

In the past, Germany government had established tourism survey analysis to analyze survey data in order to arrive at reliable conclusions on future trends in travel behavior. To aim to find how demographic change will influence the tourism market and how the industry can adapt to those changes. The travel analysis provided data on tourism consumer behavior, including attitudes, motives and intentions. Since, 1970 year, it is based on a random sample, representative for the population in private households aged 14 years or older. Then, a continuous high scientific standard combined with a national and international users makes the travel analysis a useful tool and reliable source for tourism industry and policy decisions. It aimed to gather statistical data. e.g. on the age structure and on demographic trends, quantitative and qualitative analysis with time series data from the travel analysis. It shows e.g. not only the future volume , quite different from today's seniors, or how who will travel of family holidays will change, e.g. single parents of low, but grandparents of growing significance for tourism.

Demographic change is said to be one of the important drivers for new trends in consumer traveling change behavior in most European countries (e.g. Lind 2001). Because the growing number of senior citizens in the European Union and other industralised countries, such as the USA and Japan, looks to become one of the major marketing challenges for the tourism industry. United Nations statistics predict that the share of people being 60 age or older will grow dramatically in the coming future, and is expected to rise from 10 percent of the world population in 2000 year to more than 20 percent in 2050 year (United Nations Population Division, 2001). From its statistic, some data showed that travel propensity increased throughout life until the age of about 50 years of age and was then kept stable until very late in life 75 age. The most important results is that the travel propensity when getting older is not going down between 65 and 75 age of course, the overall development of this variable is influenced by a lot of other factors which are rsponsible for quite a variation over time. It is now possible to suggest that the general pattern of travel propensity is one of the key indicators for holiday life cycle travel behaviour, includes three stages. The growth stage tends to increase from early aduithood until 45 age old or when reaching some 80%. The next stage is stabilisation from the ages of around 50 age,until 75 age old, starting with a lower increase. Finally, the decrease stage is a slight decrease occurs once people reach the more advanced age of 75 age to 85 age old (Lohmann & Danielsson 2001).

So, it seems Germany government tourism prediction to future travellers' behaviour indicated these findings, such as on how future senior generations will travel, who had used survey data to examine the patterns of travel behaviour of a generation getting older and applied the findings to draw conclusions on the future. Also, it predicted that on the future of family trips, family semgmentation will be the travel behaviour patterns in the future. These findings together with the statistical data on demographic change allowed for a better understanding of the coming tends in family holidays. It's aim developed in consumer behaviour related to demographic change and predicted what will happen future of tourism one had to consider other influences and drivers as well, for example, trends on the supply side. e.g. low cost airlines or in travelling consumption behaviour in general whether how the past may provide a key to predict travel patterns of senior sitizens to the future.

Given the projected growth of the senior citizens market, designing specific marketing strategies to meet the prospective needs of elderly tourists will become increasingly important. It has been an implict assumption that it will be a close relationship between the travel behaviour of today's senior citizens and the those of future ones. The growing number of senior citizens in the world. e.g. China, Hong Kong, Japan, USA etc. countries. Global senior citizen tourism market will be based solely on demographic predictions about the future of the population's age structure. However, many of these seniors won't only live longer but will be fitter and more active until later in life. Many of the will also have plenty in life. Many of them will also have plenty of time and money to spend on travel. So, will these new seniors behave like today's senior citizens? Will they adopt the same travel behaviour as the previous generation or become a new market of oldies for the leisure and tourism indudtry? However, to determine the actual number of senior citizens who will be travelling and to sought to evaluate and specify certain difficult to predict the actual numbers of senior citizen to any country. However, they can be based on the implicit assumption that there is a close relationship between the travel behaviour of past, present and future seniors. But is this a valid assumption? As the reiseanalyse travel analysis survey, which was conducted in Germany every year, offered some interesting data possibiltieis. It was designed to monitor the holiday travel behaviour, opinions and attitudes of Germans and has been carried out since 1970 year, questions in the questionnaire. Data are based on face to face interviews, with a representative sample of more than 7,500 repondents, the interviews being carried out in January each year. All results refer to the average for the defined generated, which ranges generally over ten years. The group of people then at the age of 60 to 69 age is described. This corresponds to the same generation ten years ago, when they had an age of 50 to 59 age. When this methodological approach is not necessarily very sophisticated, it does have the important advantages of being cost effective.

Psychological method to predict travel behavioural consumption.

On the psychological view point, I think individual traveler's character will have those kind of personal characteristics. First, simplicity searchers value above everything ease not transparency in their travel planning and holiday making, and are willing to avoid having to go through extensive research. Second, cultural purists use their travel as an opportunity to immerse themselves in an unfamiliar looking to break themselves entirely from their home lives and engage. Sincerely with a different way of living. Third, social capital seekers understand that to be well travelled is a personal quality, and their choices are shaped by their desire to take maximum of social reward from their travel. They will exploit the potential of digital media to enrich and inform their experiences, and structure their adventures always keeping in mind they are being watched by online audiences. Finally, reward hunters seek a return on the investment who make in their busy , high-achieving lives. Linked in part to the growing trend of wellness, including both physical and mental self improvement who seek truly extraordinary and often indulgent or luxurious' must have experiences.

Why needs to know the personal character of individual traveler's characteristics. Because if travel agents could feel which kinds of individual traveler's character, then who can predict which kind of travel package to design to them more easily. For example, how to determine future travel behaviour from past travel experience and perceptions of risk and safety? We need to concern that the influences of past international travel experience, types of risk associated with international travel and the overall degree of safety feeling during international travel on individual's travelling experiences likelihood of travelling to various geographic regions on their next international vacation trip or avoidance of those regions, due to perceived risk. Because individual traveler's experience of safety risk degree to the countries, it will influence who chooses to go to the countries/ country to travel again.

Why travellers avoid certain destinations are as relevant decision making as why who choose to go to the country(countries) to travel. Perceptions of risk and safety and travel experiences are likely to influence travel decisions; efforts to predict future travel behaviour can benefit to individual tourist's decision making. As Weber & Bottom (1989) defined risky decision is as "choices among alternatives that can be described by prodability distributions over possible outcomes" (p.114). Some psychologists judge subjective perceptions of physical reality, i.e. image of a particular tourist destination, whereas value judgement refers to the way individual rank destinations according to whose attributes. i.e. attractiveness, safety, risk etc. factors to form on overall image. So, if the individual traveler had unhappy and worried and unsafe experiences to go to where the place(country) to travel during whose vacation time before. Then, this negative travel experience will influence who is afraid to go to the place (country) to travel again. Risk of place, country, destination or region means the danger is relatively high to the place, ie. increasing in airplane accidents, crime or terrorist activity targeting citizens of potential traveler's nationality or the probability of occurrence is great , ie. recent occurrences involving travel regions/destinations under consideration or effective actions to control consequences exist. i.e. selecting safe regions and destinations, taking extra precautions when traveling to risky destinations. These risk factors will influence the individual traveler who chooses to cancel travel plan to go to the country again.

Another interesting research, how to predict behavioural intention of choosing a travel destination, which has focus of toursm research for years, but the complex decision making process leading to the choice of a travel destination has not been well researched. The planned behaviour model using its core constructs, attitude, subjective norm and perceived behavioural control, with the addition of the past behavioural variable on behavioural intention of choosing a travel destination.

Understanding why people travel and what factors influence their behavioural intention of choosing a travel destination is beneficial to tourism planning and marketing. Understanding travel motivation is the push and pull model. The idea of the push and pull model is the decomposition of an individual's choice of a travel destination into two forces. The first force is the push factor that pushes an indvidual away home and attempts to develop a general desire to go somewhere else, without specifying where that may be. The second force is the pull factor, that pulls on individual toward a destination, due to a region specific travel location or perceived attractiveness of a destination. The respective push and pull factors illustrate that people travel because who are pushed by their internal motives and pulled by external forces of a destination. Nevertheless, how push and pull factors guide people's attitude and how these attributes lead to behavioural intentions of choosing a travel destination have rarely been investigated. The decision making process leading to the choice of a travel destination is a very complex process. The planned behaviour model is as a research framework to predict the behavioural intention of choosing a travel destination. The model based on the three constructs of attitude, subjective norm, and perceived behavioural control (Fishbein & Ajzen, 1975).

In conclusion, the factors can influence travelers who decide to choose to travel the country, which include personal safety was perceived to the highest motivation factors among the important factors which include, scenic beauty, cultural interests, friendliness of local people, price of trip, services in hotels and restaurants, quality and variety of food and shopping facilities and services. The factors include both push and pull. Push factors include knowledge, prestige, and enhancement of human relationship etc., whereas, the most significant pull factors include high technologic image, expenditure and accessibility etc. For example, Japanese travelers visiting Hong Kong. Push factors are such as exploration dream fulfillment and pull factors are such as benefits sought, attractions and good climate city. It will be the factor of future travel patterns and motivations of sub-cultural and ethic groups for Japanese choice to go to Hong Kong travelling.

Bibliography

Backman, K., Backman, S., Uysal, M. And Sunshine, K. (1995). Event Tourism : An Examination Of Motivations And Activities. Festival Management And Event Tourism, 3(1), 15-24.

Fishbein, M., & Ajzen, Z. (1975). Belief, Attitude, Intention And Behaviour: An Introduction To Theory And Research, Boston: Addison Wesley.

Hsu, C.H.C., Cai , L.A., Li, M(2010). Expectation, Motivation And Attitude: A Tourist Behavioral Model. Journal Of Travel Research, 49(3),

282-296. http://dx.doi, org/10.1177/004728750 9349266.

ICT Information And Communication Technology Switzerland, 2005. ICT Fakten (ICT facts).

Available from http://www.ictswitzerland.ch/de/ict%2fakten/ factsfigures.asp(retrieved Dec.12, 2005) in German.

Lind, (2001): Befolkningen, Familjen, Livscykeln- Och Ekonomisk Tillvaxt. Institutet For Tillvaxtpo-litiska studier/Vinnova/Nutek.

Lohmann, Martin (2001): The 31 st. Reiseanalyse-RA 2001. Tourism: vol. 49, no.1/2001;pp.65-67, Zagreb.

United Nations Population Division (2001). World Population Prospects: The 2000 year Revision, New York.

Weber E.U., & W, P.Bottom (1989). "Axiomatic

Measures Of Perceived Risk: Some Tests And extensions." journal of behavioral decision making, 2 (2): 113-31.

Cultural distance on satisfaction and respect travel intention

Every country cultural difference is different. How and why cultural difference has a real impact on tourist satisfaction and it can also influence to repeat travel. Is cultural tourism one major factor to influence tourist to repeat travelling intention or choice to the country in international tourism choice market? For example, China and India have similar culture. Their cultural difference is not much, e.g. eating cultural habit is similar , entertainment cultural habit is similar. These both countries people do not want to spend much money in eating and entertainment both aspects. Hence, these two countries people do not consider how to consume to enjoy entertainment and eat expensive food. Hence, it is based on cultural similar reason. These both countries tourists will prefer to choose to repeat travelling either China or India. When the Indian tourists had chosen to go to China to travel in the first time. Then, the Indian tourists will choose to go to China to travel in second time again. Also, the Indian tourists had chosen to go to China to travel in first time. Then, the Chinese tourists will choose to go to India to travel in second time again.

What factors influence China and India tourists respect to travel between these both countries. The factors will include cheap air ticket price, cheap hotel living price , less economic cost factor. However, I believe the similar cultural factor will be the major factor to influence many Chinese and Indian tourist prefer to choose to repeat travelling between these both countries.

As my indication to these both countries people have similar eating habits, choosing foods, low health foods, common foods choice eating at cheap restaurant habitual consumption. Also, they have similar entertainment habits, their entertainment demand is not high. They like to ride bicycles to go to anywhere to travel. They like to go to swim, play basketball, football etc. sports. These all sports are cheap sport consumption. So, it based on similar individual low enjoyment demand and low health, food quality demand similar cultural factors. Chinese and Indian people have no long distance cultural difference between eating and entertainment habitual factor will include them to choose to repeat travelling between these both countries. Due to China and India have many restaurants can provide cheap food or sport service providers can provide different kinds of cheap sport entertainment consumption to satisfy their cheap food and cheap entertainment needs in their journey in China or India anywhere. So, it explains that why these both countries tourists will repeat to travel these both countries again after they had visited China or India to travel in first time. So, the similar cultural factor can impact these both countries tourists to repeat to go to these both countries to travel again. Hence, if these two countries' cultural distance is far or different, then themselves countries' tourists won't choose to repeat travel between themselves when these two countries for cultural distance tourists had visited to another country in first time. Hence, culture has been continuously considered as a much factor which tourists consider in terms of choice of the destination travelling place. Also, it explains cultural distance which can make tourist individual has less satisfaction to concern to tourists to repeat travels.

Otherwise, for far cultural distance two countries case example, such as Chinese and American , these two countries people's eating habit and entertainment cultural needs are different. For eating habit difference example, American like to eat pork, beefs, chickens, potato to replace rice and other foods. Otherwise, Chinese like to wat rice, vegetables more than potatoes, pork , beefs for lunch , dinner . So , their eating habits are very different. Also, American like to drive boats on the season drive cars to go to anywhere to travel on holidays for sports or holiday entertainment activities . Otherwise, Chinese like to play basketball, football, ride bicycle of cheaper sport entertainment on holidays. So, American entertainment activities are more expensive to compare Chinese. Also, US and China , like families whose power distance is different, such as every per family powerful member is parents, who have more power to give opinions to choose anywhere to travel for whose sons and/or daughters whole family members travelling arrangement.

Therefore, if the Us family powerful members, such as at least one son or/and daughter members who need t choose to go to which country to travel if the family powerful members, such as the child/ children's parent feel China's food taste or entertainment activities are totally different to be similar to their country's food taste and entertainment activities habitually after their whole family members had travelled to China in first time before. Although, their son(s) and daughter(s) will hope to go to China to repeat travel again. But, due to the US family parents are their son(s) and daughter(S) powerful decider to make any travelling decision to choose which country will be next time travelling destination. If their parents feel China's eating and entertainment culture is totally different to their countries. Then, the US family will not choose to repeat travel to the China country again any more easily, because this US family can not feel satisfactory when they visited China in their first time before, due to they feel China 's food and entertainment cultures are totally different to their US country. So, the cultural distance factor will influence the US family don't choose China to go repeat travel again.

Consequently, different countries' similar or different cultural factor will influence the country's tourists choose to repeat travel to the country again. So, any country needs to know what its culture is in order to attract the similar cultural countries tourists to repeat travel to itself country more easily.

Lifestyle factor influences travel
behavior

Whether do different countries tourists' different lifestyle which can influence their travel consumption behaviors? Even, which countries that they will choose to go to travel. For example, when one tourist who owns himself/herself often to drive to go to anywhere habitually. The tourist's driving car habital behavior which will influence that he /she will feel need to rent car to travel to anywhere habitually , when he/she selects to go to the country to travel. Hence, if he/she feels the tourism destination has no any rent car service providers to provide him/her to rent any car to travel anywhere in the country's travel destination. Does the country lack rent car service factor which will influence that he/she will still choose to go to the country to travel in preference? For example, when one New

Zealander's family who own at least one car at home. So, the New Zealand whole family every member can often drive car to go to anywhere , even, one family member had driven one car to leave his/her home. So, driving own car activity or behavior has been one habitual activity to influence the New Zealand every member to feel the travelling destination needs have rent car service provider supplies cars to let them to rent to travel. The driving car lifestyle has caused the whole New Zealander family driving habit. When the family's sons) and/or daughter(s) need(s) to go to school or go to shopping as well as their parents also need to drive their cars to go to office to work in themselves home town often. In common, there are many New Zealanders who will have at least one car at home because they feel that they can drive their themselves cars to go to anywhere in New Zealand more than waiting bus or tram or train or ferry etc. public transportation tools more conveniently. So, New Zealanders' driving own car habit will influence their lifestyle to feel that they also need to rent cars to travel to go to any where to travel to replace to wait public transportation tools choice in the travelling destination during their journey.

For shopping trips is more influenced by their driving car activities. So, it seems that this New Zealander families will be influenced to their tourism destination need, they need the tourism destination has car renting service provider to be supplied anywhere to let them can drive the renting cars to go to anywhere in tourism destination. It means that when the tourism destination has less rent car providers can provide renting car services to drive anywhere or it has none any renting car service providers are existing in the tourism destination. Then, the renting car service providers number shortage or none any renting car service providers to be provided to the country's tourism destination, which will cause the New Zealander families do not prefer to choose to go to the country to travel generally, e.g. Hong Kong, China, Korea these Asia countries have no many rent car service providers in these countries. So, the New Zealand families won't prefer to choose to go these countries to travel when they discover these Asia countries lack enough rent car service providers to let them to drive to travel in themselves conveniently. Otherwise, America, England, Japan etc. countries have many rent car service providers. So, these countries will be this New Zealander families' preferable tourism countries. Thus, the New Zealand families' driving ownership car lifestyle will influence their travel behaviors to choose to go to the country which can have many rent car providers in the tourism country any where tourism destinations in preference.

Thus, whether the country has renting car service providers , it will be variable factor to influence any country's car ownership families' driving car travel behaviors in their journey in order to let they feel that they can drive themselves ownership cars to go to anywhere to travel conveniently, even when they leave their countries. Hence, these countries' car ownership driving habitual families' behaviors will be influenced their tourism destination or location decision choice when the country has many renting car service providers in preference as well as this renting car service provider supplying factor will be more important to influence the habitual driving own car traveller to be preferable choice to compare other factors, e.g. cheap entertainment consumption providers factor which include cheap hotel living fee, cheap food price consumption etc. expenditure in the travelling country.

Thus, it explains that different countries' car ownership tourists , whose driving own car activities will cause their daily lifestyles, then their daily driving own car lifestyles will influence their tourism destination choices indirectly. So, it seems that lifestyle can be a outcome variable (or dependent variable) factor to influence travel behavior in any travelling built environment. The travelling built environment characteristics can include density measures (population density, job density), job-housing density). These travelling built environment factor can represent what the city resident's lifestyle. For example, where the location in relation to local center or regional center to the country's residents are living. This country resident's living location will cause this country resident's lifestyles , e.g. holiday or leisure whether it is low budget, active and adventurous or frequent traveller with second place or self-organized , family oriented or close to home. Hence, the country's living built environment will influence the country's resident's lifestyles. Due to different countries' residents will have different lifestyles. Hence, built environments and life styles have relationship to influence every country's residents when they need to go to other countries to travel in their holidays. For example, frequent travellers are usually living in big and busy cities, otherwise, non -frequent travellers are usually living in the country sides, where there are less offices or factories are built to let people to work. So, big city will bring busy feeling to the country's residents, then they will be influenced to feel need to often to go to travel for leisure intention in their holidays. Otherwise, countryside will bring not busy or quiet environment feeling to the country's residents, then they won't feel working feeling when they are living in county side. So, they won't feel need to go t o anywhere to travel in their holidays often.

Hence, built environment will bring either busy or not busy (quiet environment feeing) to the both different country residents when they are living in the places. Their living places will cause their lifestyles are different. Then, they will be influences to feel have more frequent travelling needs or less frequent travelling needs to explain why every country people will have more or less frequent travelling needs.

How any why peer-to-peer
accommodation can impact
business tourism pattern

I shall explain how any why peer-to-peer accommdation can attract business tourisms to choose business tourism intention? Usually , employees or employers buy business trips, why they choose one particular travelling company over another and why the business tourists choose to travel when the peer (more than one business tourists) who will choose to peer-to-per accommodation business tourism pattern more than the more expensive hotel living comfortable feeling business tourism pattern.

Business travel agents need to know or understand what reasons the employer or employee feels peer-to-peer accommodation business tourism motivation is more suitable or better to compare hotel living comfortable feeling business tourism pattern. Why can business tourism accommodation choice factor influence the business tourist's business trip choice.

Business trip means work related travel to an irregular place or work and it represents that one employee or more than on employees business tourists whose expenses are paid by the business ,he or she or they work(s) for. So, in employer's business trip expense view point, he/she expects the employee or employees can choose the most cheap expenses for whose business trip. It also means that the employer does not expect that it is a high quality journey for the employee's or employees' business trip. The business tourism is year-round, peaking in spring and autumn , but still with high levels of activity in the summer and winter months. It may be long time or short time, e.g. less than one month or more than one month, even more than half year for the business trip. When the employee is employees are working permanent full time employment. It is not for leisure intention, it means that the employer does not hope employee or employees spend(s) extra more expense to spend any leisure or goes (go) to any destinations to visit in their/her/his whole business trip.

Hence, it is based on the cheap expenses for the business trip aim, employer usually demands employees or employees to choose the peer-to-peer be cheaper accommodation to live or the employer will help its employee(s) to choose the peer-to-peer cheaper accommodation to live. So, it seems that expensive hotel living facilities won't be the preferable accommodation choice for employer because the business trip pay or reimburse the employee. Hence, business travel agencies ought not help the business tourists to choose expensive travel package, e.g. expensive hotel accommodation on the trip, expensive transportation tools, e.g. taxi renting service to get to business meetings, the cheap peer-to-peer cheap hostel accommodation and cheap transportation tool, e.g. travel buses pre-booking service, or cheap restaurant choice vacation incentives package is more attractive to let them/him/her to choose for their/her/his business trip.

A business person or a peer-to-peer business people also have /her expect to take advantage of frequent flyer schemes which allow him/her/them to take leisure trip with airlines when they/he/she is /are accumulated sufficient miles in the cheap or air ticket(s) to catch air plane for business trip. Hence, he/she /they expect(s) to earn airlines expenses from whose frequent flyer schemes when they/he/she can claim to original air ticket price from whose employer, but in fact, peer-to-peer business tourists or individual business tourist pay lesser air ticket charge from whose frequent flying program accumulated sufficient miles, even no any payment. So, airlines can benefit the business traveller, such as improved in competition millages programs, quick check in and online check in, lounges with broadband connection etc. service.

Why does peer-to-peer accommodation living factor is the most influential to any business tourist(s) to choose the travel agent? In employer's business trip expensive view point, if it has many employees need to go to other countries business trips for long days frequently. Then, the employer will consider whether the every day accommodation living cost is expensive or not. So, comparison hotel and peer-to-peer hotel price, hotel accommodation price is usually higher than small accommodation rent price. When peer-to-peer accommodation has been shown to positively impact to business trip employers in popular. Because any business spending will be one important considerable factor to influence employers to choose. However, the accommodation renting price will be more influential to impact business tourism cost. Hence, employers will estimate every whole business trip expenses how it can impact peer-to-peer or hotel accommodation choice. So, the living budget factor will be one important influential factor to influence any employers how to choose where are the suitable destination for every individual business tourist or peer-to-peer group business tourists to live. So, it seems small size peer-to-peer accommodation are compared to large size expensive hotels more suitable for business tourists.

Although, it is possible that individual employee or a group peer-to-peer employees will feel peer-to-peer accommodation is not more safe than hotel accommodation. But, their/his/her employer usually does not consider safety, comfortable environment issue for their/his/her every business trip. They only consider lose accommodation price issue. So, the accommodation choice will be one critical factor to influence employers how to help their individual employee or a group peer-to-peer employees to choose where he/she/they will live when he/she/they arrive(s) the destination for whose every business trip. Hence, it seems that accommodation will be one critical factor to influence anywhere to be chosen to live for any business trips to their individual employee or group peer-to-peer employees' needs.

Factors influence local tourists'
destination choice

What are the main internal and external factors to influence local tourist's domestic travelling choice behaviors and destination choice decision making? What are the social , cultural , personal psychological factors to influence the decision-making of local tourists to travel to different types of tourism destinations in domestic travelling destinations, e.g. attractions, available amenities, image price external factors. They can influence local tourist's destination choice behaviors. Does the individual occupational reason can influence local tourist's local destination travelling choice? So, any travel agents need to develop and promote of domestic destination need to determine the factors influencing tourist's destination choice.

In a local destination tourist individual productive way, how local tourism agents can bring what factors to influence or charge whose local destination travelling behavioral changes. For example, tourist individual behavior and destination choice factor, the comparison between the current local tourism destinations choice and the past local tourism destinations choice factor. Instead of local different travelling destination prices comparison, journeys comparison . What are the other internal and external factor to influence the local tourist's travelling destinations choices behaviors, e.g. attending local festivals, events, taste local cuisine and be part of unique features of a destination. These will be valuable external or internal factors to influence the local tourist's local destinations choices. So, different countries' local travelling destinations will need have a number of key elements that attract visitors and meet their needs. The key elements may include , for example, primary activities, physical setting and social / cultural attributes primary external activities elements, and secondary elements may include catering and shopping, and addition elements/accessibility and tourists information providing to local tourists.

Due to local destination tourism must be cheaper than overseas or foreign destination tourism. So, the local tourist travel agents need to provide their travelling services to local tourists, more attractions, accessibility , amenities, excellent available packages activities and ancillary services to compare overseas tourism destinations. Because the local tourists will compare the overseas different destinations travelling places to decide whether they ought choose to travel overseas or local different destinations at the moment. So, any entertainment activities concern local destinations which will be local tourists' preferable comparative travelling services to the local travel agent and the overseas travelling service in order to decide whether he/she ought choose local travelling or overseas travelling at the moment.

Hence, local different travelling destinations attractive factor will be one important influential factor to influence local tourist's travelling choices. However, a tourist's attitude, decisions, activities, ideas or travelling experiences evaluating and searching of any tourism service behaviors will influence the final travelling destination choice decision whether he/she ought choose to go to overseas or local travel. He/she will consider how to spend time and money and effort to carry on any kinds of entertainment activities in whose local or overseas journeys. So, the different destination local and overseas internal travelling price and spending entertainment time in journey and spending effort to arranging every travelling entertainment which every will be one considerable issue to compare budget to overseas and local different travelling destinations. If the tourist feel whose country , e.g. American's local travelling destination budget is spend less than overseas travelling destination too much. Then, the American will choose to local travelling destinations more than overseas travelling destinations and the moment. So, travelling budget will one factor to influence the tourist to choose whether overseas or local travelling.

So, it seems that time, money and effort will be another factor to influence the tourist will be another factor to influence the tourist chooses to go to overseas or local travelling destinations, instead of different travelling entertainment provider choices factor in the local or overseas travelling destinations . Moreover, the tourist's individual income, the local and overseas living condition, formation of cultural and aesthetic tastes, price of local and overseas travelling service and discounts, local and overseas travelling destinations' temperature or weather viable, e.g. number of sunny days, geographical condition, cultural and natural resource, medical tourism etc. external factors will influence the tourist individual final travelling decision to choose either local tourism or overseas tourism entertainment decision.

Tourist individual driving behavior

how to impact travel behavior

Does every tourist individual driving behavior influence whose travel behavioral choice? However, individual mobility decisions are possible difficulties for measures aiming at tourist individual travelling behavioral changes and links them to the transport need aspect when the tourist arrives the destination to travel. For example, whether the travelling destination has bus public transportation tool supplies or ferry transportation tool supplies or taxi transportation tool supplied or train or tram etc. different public transportation tools to influence the tourist individual travelling destination choice.

When every country decides to develop travel industry. It needs to understand how to arrange what kind of public transportation tools to be supplied to satisfy any countries' tourists mobility needs in whose journeys in order to achieve tourism planning for public transportation system to attract different countries' tourists to choose to arrive itself different destinations to travel more easily. So, the country's transportation services supplies will have permanently impacted to every tourist individual travel behavior towards more mobility when he/she arrives to the country to travel.

Can transportation system factor influence tourist individual travelling destination decision? it depends on the tourist individual attitude or transport needs of decisions. For example, if the city , e.g. New York has many tourists, who are high income, young gender, high education level tourists. Then, they will choose more expensive and comfortable train more than cheap and not comfortable bus transportation tool. So, I assume that the year has many high income, high education , high social class occupation tourists arrive US , New York city . Then, they will choose train more than bus transportation tool to go to anywhere to travel in New York city. So, it is not represent that the city has many cheaper public transportation tool, such as many buses number to be supplied , the bus public transportation tool can bring more income to attract overseas tourists to come to New York travel. It depends on whether the tourist individual characteristics, e.g. high or low income, more or less comfortable transporation tool supplies needs or high or low educational level, alone tourist or family tourist or friend relationship tourist. Any one of these tourist individual psychological factors will influence the tourist to choose either cheap and less comfortable public tool system or expensive and more comfortable public tool system to be supplied to the city to travel. So, the city's comfortable or not comfortable public transportation tool supplies which will influence the overseas tourists how to choose the city to travel.

However, on the tourist's habitual behavior of catching which kind of transportation tools, this factor will bring to influence how to choose the kind of transportation tool(s) whether the city can provide choice to let the overseas tourist to make where travelling decision when he/she arrives to the country. However, his/her transportation tool catching habit will be possible to influence whose travel times for public transport use, instead of which kind of transport tool(s) he/she will choose to catch when he/she arrives the country to travel.

In conclusion, the tourist's age, income, occupation, education level will influence how the tourist's transportation choice in himself/herself country, then it also bring this question: will influence the tourist individual destination choice if the country can provide or can not provide the kind of public transportation tool(s) to let the tourist to choose to catch in his/her journey in the country's city. Hence, it explains that why every country's pubic transporation tool supplies will influence the tourist to choose where to travel in the country.

What are usually travel behaviors and attitudes to disabled tourists

What factors can affect the travel behaviors of people with disabilities by ages and lifestyle variable factors? When one person is disable, he/she will have different behaviors to satisfy whose needs in whose whole travelling journey. In special , the older age and younger age disable tourists who will have different travelling needs. In fact, the disabled tourists won't easy to go anywhere travelling destinations in whose whole travelling journey. So, it seems that the travelling entertainment needs won't be very much to these younger or older disabled tourists. Moreover, people with disabilities travel will be compare with people without disabilities. So, it is one key to explain why the travelling entertainment purposes or needs to disable people which are lesser than the people without disabilities.

In negative or problematic experience of travel to disabled tourists aspect, I believe that it is one travelling experiences problem is considered to need to be solved to any younger or older age disabled tourists, because they are handicapped people, they will feel walk in difficulty, even they need wheel chairs to help them to walk. So, the moving disabled problem will influence how they feel unsafe on public transport in any strange travelling countries considerable. In special, the older aged 50 and over disabled people need to catch any public transport when they need to sit on wheel chairs to go to anywhere destinations in any strange travelling countries. They will feel not convenient and unsafe when they need to sit on wheel chairs to go to anywhere destinations. These travelling places are their first time arriving places. Hence, transportation tools will be consideration problem to any disabled tourists. It seems that renting car travelling providers will be one popular or preferable choice to any younger orolder age disabled tourists. Because disabled tourists won't need to catch public transport tools, such as buses, trains, trams, taxis in unsafe, notconvenient natural travelling environment. They can drive themselves renting cars to go to anywhere travelling destinations easily or conveniently. Thus, I believe that the renting cr travelling service which is very attractive to any young or old age disabled tourist nowadays.

In general, instead of renting cars to drive behavioral change to disabled tourists usually ,renting cars behaviors which will replace to choose to catch any public transportation tools behavior to disable tourists. What kinds of other behavioral changes will impact to disabled tourists? Other aspect consideration is disabled tourist individual health problem . For example, if the disabled tourist is driving himself/herself renting cars to go to anywhere destinations in long term in the travelling country. The long distance of driving miles travelling and driving long hours spend travelling behaviors will influence the disable tourist individual nervous health to be more poor, because he/she needs to spend more time and nervous to drive whose renting car to go to anywhere in whole travelling journey. So, it is very dangerous and unsafe to the disabled tourist when he/she needs to concentrate on nervous to drive himself/herself renting car to go to anywhere destinations to travel in whose travelling journey or trip.

In consideration of the older age disabled tourist groups will be more unsafe and dangerous when he/she needs to spend much time to drive whose renting car to arrive any travelling destinations. So, it is based on this long time unsafe driving factor, the older age disabled tourist groups will choose to spend lesser time to drive to go to anywhere destinations to travel alone or with their friends and/or families in general. Similar patterns are evident in the numbers of miles travelled and the time spent to driving renting car behavior to any older age disabled tourist groups will be lesser than the younger age disabled tourist groups . Due to the long time unsave renting car self-driving feeling to the older age disabled tourists. It will impact to influence the older age disabled tourists to choose to catch any public transport or walking to replace renting car self-driving behaviors in their trips, when older age handicapped tourists loss hearing, sight, memory, recognizing physical danger, personal care difficulties disabled characteristics.

Thus, the long time renting car driving behavior which will influence the old age disabled tourists to choose to catch public transport tools to replace to rent car to drive in whose trip persuasively. So, the renting car providers will have lesser old age disable tourist number to compare to young age disabled tourist number in common. Also, the old age disable tourists will prefer to choose the travel destinations where have many public transport tools to let them to catch for their travelling journeys.

How social internet networking
impacts traveller individual behavior

Can web site online internet networking influence traveller individual behavior changes? If web site can influence every online traveller user individual behavior change, how it influence every online user individual behavior change in order to impact his/her travelling service or arrangement change choice. For example, when the traveller walks in one travel agent's shop to find the most suitable travelling package for whose trip.

At the moment, he/she plans to find the travel agent to help him/her to arrange any travelling package. But when he/she goes back his/her home, he/she turns on his/her computer to link online travel agent website. Then, he/she discovers this online travel agent can provide more attractive travelling package similar service and he/she will compare the walk in travel agent's travelling package to this online travel agent travelling package. Although, the walk-in travelling agent can provide lesser service fee to compare this online travel agent. But , he/she feels this online travel agent can provide more attractive and enjoyable travelling entertainment and trip arrangement service to satisfy his/her travelling need. So, he/she decides to choose this online travelling agent's travelling package and it seems that the online travel agent web site can influence his/her original travelling agent target choice.

Nowadays, the most famous online development reshaping traditional marketing methods of tourism business will be possible to replace the traditional walk-in travel agent business. Because travelling consumers like to turn on computer to link to different travelling agents' websites to choose which travelling package is the cheapest or it can provide the most attractive or enjoyable entertainment arrangement in the trip. So, online travel agents will influence travelling consumers to reduce to spend time to walk in to visit any travel agent shops. The traveller prefers to spend much time to find which travelling agents' websites to find the most right online travelling agent to help him/her to arrange the trip service to replace to find the most right walk-in travelling agent at home conveniently. So, travelling agent website development can impact every traveller individual planning behavior to be changed influentially because when he/she plans to walk in to visit the identified travel agent shop, but when he/she has one desk top computer to be installed at home. Then, he/she will have another choice to buy the travelling package service. So, he/she will change his/her walk in to visit the travel agent planning behavior to change to clicking on any travel agent's website behavior.

Moreover, travelling website characteristics or attractive point is easy communication. When the traveller feels any worry or trouble, he/her need to enquire the online travelling agent immediately. He/she can send email to enquire the travelling agent to arrange travelling package similar service to walk in travel agent and he/she will compare the walk in travel agent's travelling package to this online travel agent travelling package. Although, the walk-in travelling agent can provide lesser service fee to compare this online travel agent. But, he/she feels that this online travel agent can provide more attractive and enjoyable travelling entertainment and trips service to satisfy his/her travelling need. So, he/she decides to choose this online travelling agent's travelling package and it seems that the online travel agent website can influence his/her original travelling agent target choice.

Nowadays, the most famous online development reshaping traditional marketing methods of tourism business will be possible to replace the traditional walk-in travel agent business. Because travelling walk-in consumer like to turn on computer to link to different travelling agents' websites to choose which travelling package is the cheapest or it can provide the most attractive or enjoyable entertainment arrangement .

Thus, online travelling information search tool can attract travellers to choose to find any travel agents' websites from internet to replace walk-in travel agents' shops influentially. Also, it seems online travelling service will be popular to replace walk-in travelling service in possible.

● Culture
intentionral distance on satisfaction and
respect travel

Every country cultural difference is different. How and why cultural difference has a real impact on tourist satisfaction and it can also influence to repeat travel. Is cultural tourism one major factor to influence tourist to repeat travelling intention or choice to the country in international tourism choice market? For example, China and India have similar culture. Their cultural difference is not much, e.g. eating cultural habit is similar , entertainment cultural habit is similar. These both countries people do not want to spend much money in eating and entertainment both aspects. Hence, these two countries people do not consider how to consume to enjoy entertainment and eat expensive food. Hence, it is based on cultural similar reason. These both countries tourists will prefer to choose to repeat travelling either China or India. When the Indian tourists had chosen to go to China to travel in the first time. Then, the Indian tourists will choose to go to China to travel in second time again. Also, the Indian tourists had chosen to go to China to travel in first time. Then, the Chinese tourists will choose to go to India to travel in second time again.

What factors influence China and India touists repect to travel between these both countries. The factors will include cheap air ticket price, cheap hotel living price , less economic cost factor. However, I believe the similar cultural factor will be the major factor to influence many Chinese and

Indian tourist prefer to choose to repeat travelling between these both countries.

As my indication to these both countries people have similar eating habits, choosing foods, low health foods, common foods choice eating at cheap restaurant habitual consumption. Also, they have similar entertainment habits, their entertainment demad is not high. They like to ride bicycles to go to anywhere to travel. They like to go to swim, play backetball, football etc. sports. These all sports are cheap sport consumption. So, it based on similar individual low enjoyment demand and low health, food quality demand similar cultural factors. Chinese and Indian people have no long distance cultural difference between eating and entertainment habitual factor will include them to choose to repeact travelling between these both countries. Due to China and India have many restaurants can provide cheap food or sport service providers can provide diffent kinds of cheap sport entertainment consumption to satisfy their cheap food and cheap entertainment needs in their journey in China or India anywhere. So, it explains that why these both countries tourists will repeat to travel these both countries again after they had visited China or India to travel in first time. So, the similar cultural factor can impact these both countries tourists to repeat to go to these both countries to travel again. Hence, if these two countries' cultural distance is far or different, then themselves countries' tourists won't choose to repeat travel between themselves when these two countries for cultural distance toutists had visited to another country in first time. Hence, culture has been continuously considered as a much factor which tourists consider in terms of choice of the destination travelling place. Also, it explains cultural distance which can make tourist individual has less satisfaction to concern to tourists to repeat travels.

Otherwise, for far cultural distance two countries case example, such as Chinese and American , these two countries people's eating habit and entertainment cultural needs are different. For eating habit difference example, American like to eat poks, beefs, chickens, potatos to replace rice and other foods. Otherwise, Chinese like to wat rice, vegatables more than potatoes, porks , beefs for lunch , dinner . So , their eating habits are very different. Also, American like to drive boats on the seasor drive crs to go to anywhere to travel on holidays for sports or holiday entertainment activities . Otherwise, Chinese like to play backetball, football, ride bicycle of cheaper sport entertainment on holidays. So, American entertainment activities are more expensive to compare Chinese. Also, US and China , like families whose power distance is dfferent, such as every per family powerful member is parents, who have more power to give opinions to choose anywhere to travel for whose sons and/or daughters whole familily members travelling arrangement.

Therefore, if the Us family powerful members, such as at least one son or/ and ond daughter members who need t choose to go to which country to travel if the family powerful members, such as the child/ children's parent feel China's food taste or entertainment activities are totally different to be similar to their country's food taste and entertainment activities habitually after their whole fmily members had travelled to China in first time before. Although, their son(s) and daughter(s) will hope to go to China to repect travel again. But, due to the US family parents are their son(s) and daughter(S) powerful decider to make any travelling decision to choose which country will be next time travelling destination. If their parents feel China's eating and entertainment culture is totally different to their countries. Then, the US family will not choose to repeat travel to the China country again any more easily, beause this US family can not feel satisfactory when they visited China in their first time before, due to they feel China 's food and entertainment cultures are totally different to their US country. So, the cultural distance factor will influence the US family don't choose China to fo repeat travel again.

Consequently, different countries' similar or different cultural factor will influence the country's tourists choose to repeact travel to the country again. So, any country needs to know what its culture is in order to attract the similar cultural countries tourists to repeat travel to itself country more easily.

Lifestyle factor influences travel
behavior

Whether do different countries tourists' different lifestyle which can influence their travel consumption behaviors? Even, which countries that they will choose to go to travel. For example, when one tourist who owns himself/herself often to drive to go to anywhere habitually. The tourist's driving car habital behavior which will influence that he /she will feel need to rent car to travel to anywhere habitually , when he/she selects to go to the country to travel. Hence, if he/she feels the tourism destination has no any rent car service providers to provide him/her to rent any car to travel anywhere in the country's travel destination. Does the country lack rent car service factor which will influence that he/she will still choose to go to the country to travel in preference? For example, when one New Zealander's family who own at least one car at home. So, the New Zealand whole family every member can often drive car to go to anywhere , even, one family member had driven one car to leave his/her home. So, driving own car activity or behavior has been one habitual activity to influence the New Zealand every member to feel the travelling destination needs have rent car service provider supplies cars to let them to rent to travel. The driving car lifestyle has caused the whole New Zealander family driving habit. When the family's sons) and/or daughter(s) need(s) to go to school or go to shopping as well as their parents also need to drive their cars to go to office to work in themselves home town often. In common, there are many New Zealanders who will have at least one car at home because they feel that they can drive their themselves cars to go to anywhere in New Zealand more than waiting bus or tram or train or ferry etc. public transportation tools more conveniently. So, New Zealanders' driving own car habit will influence their lifestyle to feel that they also need to rent cars to travel to go to any where to travel to replace to wait public transportation tools choice in the travelling destination during their journey.

For shopping trips is more influenced by their driving car activities. So, it seems that this New Zealander families will be influenced to their tourism destination need, they need the tourism destination has car renting service provider to be supplied anywhere to let them can drive the renting cars to go to anywhere in tourism destination. It means that when the tourim destination has less rent car providers can provide renting car services to drive anywhere or it has none any renting car service providers are existing in the tourism destination. Then, the renting car service providers number shortage or none any renting car service providers to be provided to the country's tourism destination, which will cause the New Zealander families do not perfer to choose to go to the country to travel generally, e.g. Hong Kong, China, Korea these Asia countries have no many rent car service providers in these countries. So, the New Zealand families won't prefer to choose to go these countries to travel when they discover these Asia countries lack enough rent car service providers to let them to drive to travel in themselves conveniently. Otherwise, America, England, Japan etc. countries have many rent car service providers. So, these countries will be this New Zealander families' preferable tourism countries. Thus, the New Zealand families' driving ownership car lifestyle will influence their travel behaviors to choose to go to the country which can have many rent car providers in the tourism country any where tourism destinations in preference.

Thus, whether the country has renting car service providers , it will be variable factor to influence any country's car ownship families' driving car travel behaviors in their journey in order to let they feel that they can drive themselves ownship cars to go to anywhere to travel conveniently, even when they leave their countries. Hence, these countries' car ownship driving habitual families' behaviors will be influenced their tourism destination or location decision choice when the country has many renting car service providers in preference as well as this renting car service provider supplying factor will be more important to influence the habitual driving own car traveller to be preferable choice to compare other factors, e.g. cheap entertainment consumption providers factor which include cheap hotel living fee, cheap food price consumption etc. expenditure in the travelling country.

Thur, it explains that different countries' car ownship tourists , whose driving own car activities will cause their daily lifestyles, then their daily driving own car lifestyles will influence their tourism destination choices indirectly. So, it seems that lifestyle can be a outcome variable (or dependent variable) factor to influence travel behavior in any travelling built environment. The travelling built environment characteristics can include density measures (population density, job density), job-housing density). These travelling buit environment factor can represent what the city resident's lifestyle. For example, where the location in relation to local centre or regional centre to the country's residents are living. This country resident's living location will cause this country resident's lifestyles , e.g. holiday or leisure whether it is low budget, active and adventurous or frequent traveller with second place or self-orgnized , family oriented or close to home and unadventurour. Hence, the country's living built environment will influence the country's resident's lifestyles. Due to different countries' residents will have different lifestyles. Hence, built environments and lifestlyes have relationship to influence every country's residents when they need to go to other countries to travel in their holidays. For example, frequent travellers are usually living in big and busy cities, otherwise, non -frequent travellers are ususally living in the countrysides, where there are less offices or factories are built to let people to work. So, big city will bring busy feeling to the country's residents, then they will be influenced to feel need to often to go to travel for leisure intention in their holidays. Otherwise, countryside will bring not busy or quiet environment feeling to the country's residents, then they won't feel working feeling when they are living in counryside. So, they won't feel need to go t o anywhere to travel in their holidays often.

Hence, built environment will bring either busy or not busy (quiet environment feeing) to the both different country residents when they are living in the places. Their living places will cause their lifestyles are different. Then, they will be influences to feel have more frequent travelling needs or less frequent travelling needs to explain why every country people will have more or less frequent travelling needs.

● How any why peer-to-peer
accommodation can impact
business tourism pattern

I shall explain how any why peer-to-peer accomodation can attract business tourisms to choose business tourism intention? Usually , employees or employers buy business trips, why they choose one particular travelling company over another and why the business tourists choose to travel when the peer (more than one buiness tourists) who will choose to peer-to-per accommodation business tourism pattern more than the more expensive hotel living comfortable feeling business tourism pattern.

Business travel agents need to know or understand what reasons the employer or employee feels peer-to-peer accommodation business tourism motivation is more suitable or better to compare hotel living comfortable feeling business tourism pattern. Why can business tourism accommodation choice factor influence the business tourist's business trip choice.

Business trip means work related travel to an irregular place or work and it represents that one employee or more than on employees business tourists whose expenses are paid by the business ,he or she or they work(s) for. So, in employer's business trip expense view point, he/she expects the employee or employees can choose the most cheap expenses for whose business trip. It also means that the exployer does not expect that it is a high quality journey for the employee's or employees' business trip. The business tourism is year-round, peaking in spring and autumn , but still with high levels of activity in the summer and winter months. It may be long time ot short time, e.g. less than one month or more than one month, evern more than half year for the business trip. When the employee is employees are working permanent full time employment. It is not for leisure intention, it means that the employer does not hope employee or employees spend(s) extra more expense to spend any leisure or goes (go) to any destinations to visit in their/her/his whole business trip.

Hence, it is based on the cheap expenses for the business trip aim, employer usually demands employees or employees to choose the peer-to-peer be cheaper accommodation to live or the employer will help its employee(s) to choose the peer-to-peer cheaper accommodation to live. So, it seems that expensive hotel living facilities won't be the preferable accommodation choice for employer because the business trip pay or reimburse the employee. Hence, business travel agencies ought not help the business tourists to choose expensive travel package, e.g. expensive hotel accommodation on the trip, expensive transportation tools, e.g. taxi renting service to get to buisness meetings, the cheapt peer-to-peer cheap hostel accommodation and cheap transportation tool, e.g. travel buses pre-booking service, or cheap restaurant choice vacation incentives package is more attractive to let them/him/her to choose for their/her/his business trip.

A business person or a peer-to-peer business people also have /her expect to take advantage of frequent flyer schemes which allow him/her/them to take leisure trip with airlines when they/he/she is /are accumulated sufficient miles in the chep or tair ticket(s) to catch air plane for businss trip. Hence, he/she /they expect(s) to earn airlines expenses from whose frequent flyer schemes when they/he/she can claim to original air ticket price from whose employer, but in fact, peer-to-peer business tourists or individual business tourist pay lesser ait ticket charge from whose frequent flying program accumulated sufficient miles, even no any payment. So, airlines can benefit the business traveller, such as improved in competition milages programs, quick check in and online check in, lounges with broadband connection etc. service.

Why does peer-to-oeer accommodation living factor is the most influential to any business tourist(s) to choose the travel agent? In employer's business trip expensive view point, if it has many employees need to go to other countries business trips for long days frequently. Then, the employer will consider whether the every day accommodation living cost is expensive or not. So, comparison hotel and peer-to-peer hostle price, hotel accommodation price is usually higher than hostle accommodation rent price. When peer-to-peer accommodation has been shown to positively impact to business trip employers in popular. Because any business spending will be one important considerable factor to influence employers to choose. However, the accommodation renting price will be more influential to impact business tourism cost. Hence, employers will estimate every whole business trip expenses how it can impact peer-to-peer or hotel accommodation choice. So, the living budget factor will be one important influential factor to influence any employers how to choose where are the suitable destination for every individual business tourist or peer-to-peer group business tourists to live. So, it seems small size peer-to-peer hostles are compared to large size expensive hotels more suitable for business tourists.

Although, it is possible that individual employee or a group peer-to-peer employees will feel peer-to-peer hostle is not more safe than hotel accommodation. But, their/his/her employer usually does not consider safety, comfortable environment issue for their/his/her every business trip. They only consider loe accommodation price issue. So, the accommodation choice will be one critical factor to influence employers how to help their individual employee or a group peer-to-peer employees to choose where he/she/they will live when he/she/they arrive(s) the destination for whose every business trip. Hence, it seems that accommodation will be one critical factor to influence anywhere to be chosen to live for any business trips to their individual employee or group peer-to-peer employees' needs.

● Factors influence local tourists'
destination choice

What are the main internal and external factors to influence local tourist's domestic travelling choice behaviors and detination choice decision making? What are the social , cultural , personal psychological factors to influence the decision-making of local tourists to travel to different types of tourism destinations in domestic travelling destinations, e.g. attractions, available amenities, accessinility, image price external factors. They can influence local tourist's destination choice behaviors. Does the individual occupational reason can influence local tourist's local destination travelling choice? So, any travel agents need to develop and promote of domestic destination need to determine the factors influencing tourist's destination choice.

In a local destination tourist individual productive way, how loca tourism agents can bring what factors to influence or charge whose local destination travelling behavioral changes. For example, tourist individual behavior and destination choice factor, the comparision between the current local tourism destinations choice and the past local tourism destinations choice factor. Instead of local different travelling destination prices comparison, journeys comparison . What are the other internal and external factor to influence the local tourist's travelling destinations choices behaviors, e.g. attending local festivals, events, taste local cuisine and be part of unique features of a destination. These will be valuable external or internal factors to influence the local tourist's local destinatons choices. So, different countries' local travelling destinations will need have a number og key elements that attract visitors and meet their needs. The key elements may include , for example, primary activities, physical setting and social / cultural attributes primary external activities elements, and secondary elements may include catering and shopping, and addition elements/ accessibility and tourists information providing to local tourists.

Due to local destinaton tourism must be cheaper than overseas or foreigh destination tourism. So, the local torust travel agents need to provide thei travelling services to local tourists, more attractions, accessibility , amenities, excellent available packages activities and ancillary services to compare overseas tourism destinations. Because the local tourists will compare the overseas different destinations travelling places to decide whether they ought choose to travel overseas or local different destinations at the moment. So, any entertainment activities concern local destinations which will be local tourists' perferable comparative travelling services to the local travel agent and the overseas travelling service in order to decide whether he/she ought choose local travelling or overseas travelling at the moment.

Hence, local different travelling destinatons attractive factor will be one important influential factor to influence local tourist's travelling choices. However, a tourist's attitude, decisions, activities, ideas or travelling experiences evaluating and searching of any tourism service behaviors will influence the final travelling destinaton choice decision whether he/she ought choose to go to overseas or local travel. He/she will consider how to spend time and money and effort to carry on any kinds of entertainment activitied in whose local or overseas journeys. So, the different destination local and overseas internal travelling price and spending entertainment time in journey and spending effort to arranging every travelling entertainment which every will be one considerable issue to compare budget to overseas and local different travelling destinations. If the tourist feel whose country , e.g. American's local travelling destination budget is spend less than overseas travelling destination too much. Then, the American will choose to local travelling destinations more than overseas travelling destinations and the moment. So, travelling budget will one factor to influence the tourist to choose whether overseas or local travelling.

So, it seems that time, money and effort will be another factor to influence the tourist will be another factor to influence the tourist chooses to go to overseas or local travelling destinations, instead of different travelling entertainment provider choices factor in the local or overseas travelling destinations . Moreover, the tourist's indvidual income, the local and overseas living condition, formation of cultural and aesthetic tasts, price of local and overseas travelling service and discounts, loca and overseas travelling destinations' temperature or weather viable, e.g. number of sunny days, geographical condition, cultural and natural resource, medical tourism etc. external factors will influence the tourist individual final travelling decision to choose either local tourism or overseas tourism entertainment decision.

Economic environment influence driving
traveller behavior

Does every tourist individual driving behavior influence whose travel behavioral choice? However, individual mobility decisions are possible difficulties for measures aiming at tourist individual travelling behavioral changes and links them to the transport need aspect when the tourist arrivee the destination to travel. For example, whether the travelling destination has bus public transportation tool supplies or ferry transportation tool supplies or taxi transportation tool supplied ot train or tram etc. different public transportation tools to influence the tourist individual travelling destination choice.

When every country decides to develop travel industry. It needs to understand how to arrange what kind of public transportation tools to be supplied to satisfy any countries' tourists mobility needs in whose journeys in order to achieve tourism planning for public transportation system to attract different countries' tourists to choose to arrive itself different destinations to travel more easily. So, the country's transportation services supplies will have permanently impacted to every tourist individual travel behavior towards more mobility when he/she arrives to the country to travel.

Can transportation system factor influence tourist individual travelling desination decision? it depends on the tourist individual attitude or transport needs of decisions. For example, if the city , e.g. New York has many tourists, who are high income, young gender, high education level tourists. Then, they will choose more expensive and comforable train more than cheap and not comfortable bus transportation tool. So, I assume that the year has many high income, high education , high social class occupation tourists arrive US , New York city . Then, they will choose train more than bus transportation tool to go to anywhere to travel in New York city. So, it is not represent that the city has many cheaper public transportation tool, such as many buses number to be supplied , the bus public public transporation tool can bring more income to attract overseas tourists to come to New York travel. It depends on whether the tourist individual characteristics, e.g. high or low income, more or less comfortable transportion tool supplies needs or high or low educational level, alone tourist or family tourist or friend relationship tourist. Any one of these tourist individul psychological factors will influence the tourist to choose either cheap and less comfortable public tool system or expensive and more comfortable public tool system to be supplied to the city to travel. So, the city's comfortable or not comfortable public transportation tool supplies which will influence the overseas tourists how to choose the city to travel.

However, on the tourist's habitual behavior of catching which kind of transportation tools, this factor will bring to influence how to choose the kind of transportation tool(s) whether the city can provide choice to let the overseas tourist to make where travelling decision when he/she arrives to the coutry. However, his/her transporatin tool catching habit will be possible to influenc whose travel times for public transport use, instead of which kind of transport tool(s) he/she will choose to catch when he/she arrives the country to travel.

In conclusion, the tourist's age, income, occupation, education level will influence how the tourist's transportation choice in himself/herself country, then it also bring this question: will influence the tourist individual destination choice if the country can provide or can not provide the kind of public transportation tool(s) to let the tourist to choose to catch in his/her journey in the country's city. Hence, it explains that why every country's pubic transporation tool supplies will influence the tourist to choose where to travel in the country.

What are usually travel behaviors

and attitudes to disabled tourists

What factors can affect the travel behaviors of people with disabilites by ages and lifestyle variable factors? When one person is disable, he/she will have different behaviors to satisfy whose needs in whose whole travelling journey. In special , the older age and younger age disable tourists who will have diffeent travelling needs. In fact, the disabled tourists won't easy to go anywhere travelling destinations in whose whole travelling journey. So, it seems that the travelling entertainment needs won't be very much to these younger or older disabled tourists. Moreover, people with disabilities travel will be compare with people without disabilities. So, it is one key to explain why the travelling entertainment purposes or needs to disable people which are lesser than the people without disabilities.

In negative or problematic experience of travel to disabled tourists aspect, I believe that it is one travelling expereinces problem is considered to need to be solved to any younger or older age disabled tourists, because they are handicapped people, they will feel walk in difficulty, even they need wheelchaires to help them to walk. So, the visiable mving disabled problem will influence how they feel unsafe on public transport in any strange travelling countries considerabllly. In special, the older aged 50 and over disabled people need to catch any public transport when they need to sit on wheelchaires to go to anywhere destinations in any strange travelling countries. They will feel unconvenient and unsafe when they need to sit on wheelchaires to go to anywhere destinations. These travelling places are their first time arriving places. Hence, transportation tools will be consideration problem to any disabled tourists. It seems that renting car travelling providers will be one popular or preferable choice to any younger orolder age disabled tourists. Because disabled tourists won't need to catch public transport tools, such as buses, trains, trams, taxis in unsafe, unconvenient natural travelling environment. They can drive themselves renting cars to go to anywhere travelling destinations easily or conveniently. Thus, I believe that the renting cr travelling service which is very attractive to any young or old age disabled tourist nowadays.

In general, instead of renting cars to drive behavioral change to disabled tourists usually ,renting cars behaviors which will replace to choose to catch any public transportation tools behavior to disable tourists. What kinds of other behavioral changes will impact to disabled tourists? Other aspect consideration is disabled tourist individual health problem . For example, if the disabled tourist is driving himself/herself renting cars to go to anywhere destinations in long term in the travelling country. The long distance of driving miles travelling and driving long hours spend travelling behaviors will influence the disable tourist individual nervous health to be more poor, because he/she needs to spend more time and nervous to drive whose renting car to go to anywhere in whole travelling journey. So, it is very dangerous and unsafe to the disabled tourist when he/she needs to concentrate on nervous to drive himself/herself renting car to go to anywhere destinations to travel in whose travelling journey or trip.

In consideration of the older age disabled tourist groups will be mor unsafe and dangerous when he/she needs to spend much time to drive whose renting car to arrive any travelling destinations. So, it is based on this long time unsafe driving factor, the older age disabled tourit groups will choose to spend lesser time to drive to go to anywhere destinations to travel alone or with their friends and/or families in general. Similar patterns are evident in the numbers of miles travelled and the time spent to driving renting car behavior to any older age disabled tourist groups will be lesser than the younger age disabled tourist groups . Due to the long time unsae renting car self-driving feeling to the older age disabled tourists. It will impact to influence the older age disabled tourists to choose to catch any public transport or walking to replace renting car self-driving behaviors in their trips, when older age handicapped tourists loss hearing, sight, memory, recognizing physical danger, personal care difficulties disabled characteristics.

Thus, the long time renting car driving behavior which will influence the old age disabled tourists to choose to catch public transport tools to replace to rent car to drive in whose trip persuasively. So, the renting car providers will have lesser old age disable tourist number to compare to young age disabled tourist number in common. Also, the old age disable touristss will prefer to choose the travel destinations where have many public transport tools to let them to catch for their travelling journeys.

● How social internet networking
impacts driving traveler behavior

Can web site online internet networking influence traveller individual behavior changes? If web site can influence every online traveller user individual behavior change, how it influence every online user individual behavior change in order to impact his/her travelling service or arrangement change choice. For example, when the traveller walks in one travel agent's shop to find the most suitable travelling packge for whose trip. At the moment, he/she pland to find the travel agent to help him/her to arrange any travelling package. But when he/she goes back his/her home, he/she turns on his/her computer to link online travel agent website. Then, he/she discovers this online travel agent can provide more attractive travelling package similar service ans he/she will compare the walk in travel agent's travelling package to this online travel agent travelling package. Although, the walk-in travelling agent can provide lesser service fee to compare this online travel agent. But , he/she feels this online travel agent can provide more attractive and enjoyable travelling entertainment and trip arrangement service to satisfy his/her travelling need. So, he/she decides to choose this online travelling agent's travelling package and it seems that the online travel agent web site can influence his/her original travelling agent targe choice.

Nowadays, the most famous online developmet reshaping traditional marketing methods of tourism business will be possible to replace the traditional walk-in travel agent business. Because travelling consumers like to turn on computer to link to different travelling agents' websites to choose which travelling package is the cheapest or it can provie the most attractive or enjoyable entertainment arrangement in the trip. So, online travel agents will influence travelling consumers to reduce to spend time to walk in to visit any travel agent shops. The traveller prefers to spend much time to find which travelling agents' websites to find the most right online travelling agent to help him/her to arrange the trip service to replace to find the most right walk-in travelling agent at home conveniently. So, travelling agent website development can impact every traveller individual planning behavior to be changed influentially because when he/she plans to walk in to visit the identified travel agent shop, but when he/she has one desk top computer to be installed at home. Then, he/she will have another choice to buy the travelling package service. So, he/she will change his/her walk in to visit the travel agent planning behavior to change to clicking on any travel agent's website behavior.

Moreover, travelling website characteristics or attractive point is easy communication. When the traveller feels any worry or trouble, he/her need to enquire the online travelling agent immediately. He/she can send email to enquire the travelling agent to arrange travelling package similar service to walk in travel agent and he/she will compare the walk in travel agent's travelling package to this online travel agent travelling package.

Although, the walk-in travelling agent can provide lesser service fee to compare this online travel agent. But, he/she feels that this online travel agent can provide more attractive and enjoyable travelling entertainment and trips service to satisfy his/her travelling need. So, he/she decides to choose this online travelling agent's travelling package and it seems that the online travel agent website can influence his/her original travelling agent target choice.

Nowadays, the most famous online development reshaping traditional marketing methods of tourism business will be possible to replace the traditional walk-in travel agent business. Because travelling walk-in consumer like to turn on computer to link to different travelling agents' websites to choose which travelling package is the cheapest or it can provide the most attractive or enjoyable entertainment arrangement .

Thus, online travelling information search tool can attract travellers to choose to find any travel agents' websites from internet to replace walk-in travel agents' shopes influentially. Also, it seems online travelling service will be popular to replace walk-in travelling service in possible.